CW01085306

SILENCE THE IMPOSTER

WEAPONS TO SILENCE IMPOSTER SYNDROME

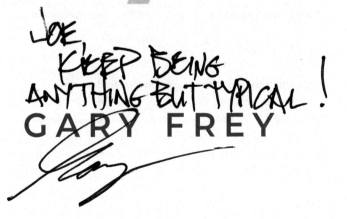

JOE,
KEEP BEING
ANYTHING BUT TYPICAL!

GARY FREY

Silence the Imposter: *7 Weapons to Silence Imposter Syndrome*

Gary Frey © 2023

All rights reserved. No part of this publication may be reproduced, distributed, or transmitted in any form by any means, including photocopying, recording, or other electronic methods without the prior written permission of the author, except in the case of brief quotations embodied in reviews and certain other noncommercial uses permitted by copyright law.

ISBN: 979-8-9890736-0-3 (Print)
ISBN: 979-8-9890736-1-0 (Ebook)

TABLE OF CONTENTS

ADVANCE PRAISE

"Gary Frey is real, and his book, *Silence the Imposter*, is even more real. This book addresses the suppressed reality of people thinking they must be someone else to succeed. Gary presents a step-by-step understanding of the process that you must apply to become and stay your true (and more powerful) self. More than a wake-up call, this book gives you a mirror to success. Your success. Read it. Study it. Implement it. Bank it."

— **Jeffrey Gitomer,**
New York Times Best-Selling Author

"Gary brings real-life lessons that all business leaders can relate to. *Silence The Imposter* showcases seven weapons that are thoughtful and relatable. I especially liked Weapons #1, #3, and #4. As a four-time serial entrepreneur, at my first company, there were so many challenges that I had never experienced, and I felt like my CEO peers had all the answers. I could have used Gary's book to show I was not alone (Weapon #1). As I moved on to launch more companies, I recognized the power of Weapon #2: Discover your Thrive/Wither Zones. As companies scale and jobs morph, this exercise helps leaders focus on what they are good at *and* gives them energy. Weapon #4 is my personal favorite. Focusing on others was a smart business decision and brought me so much joy. I highly recommend reading *Silence the Imposter* and learning about the seven Weapons!"

— Cindy Praeger, CEO,
Veranda Partners

"Silence the Imposter is illuminating for every soul grappling with the echoing whispers of self-doubt. Drawing from his own tumultuous journey and the invaluable insights from various accomplished figures, Gary Frey delicately unravels the prevalent imposter syndrome that plagues even the most seemingly confident individuals. Beyond just sharing, he equips the reader with seven formidable weapons and tools that have transformed his life and countless others. This book isn't merely an account; it's an intimate dialogue with everyone who's felt 'less than', yearning for a space to belong and thrive authentically. If you've ever felt the weight of perfectionism, battled with comparison, or questioned your worth, let this book guide you toward emancipation. Dive deep into these pages and emerge with a renewed sense of purpose and a silenced imposter. Highly recommended."

— Andy Hilliard, CEO,
Accelerance

PREFACE

In case you can relate to feeling lost or like an imposter...

One of my best friends told me these words when my world was crashing all around me: "Out of our most painful struggles often emerges our greatest blessing to others."

The question, "Where do I fit?" was a question that tormented me from the time I was a kid well into my adulthood. Unfortunately, it took me far too long to discover that I'm not alone in this. I've served and coached many CEOs and business owners in my career. I've also interviewed many on the *Anything but Typical* podcast. (You can hear their amazing stories on your favorite podcast channel here: www.abtpodcast.com.) And from all these experiences, to my great surprise, "imposter syndrome" is far more prevalent in people you'd never suspect.

While I still have moments when the imposter whispers in my ear, I've discovered seven weapons that have silenced it for me and others.

If you can relate at all, this book is for you.

The world is awash in books and information. Given the information overload in our world, I've questioned if I should go to all the effort required to write a book. My gut tells me that I'm not the only one who has wrestled with many things, such as:

- Harassed by feeling "less-than" and thinking you are alone
- Tormented with perfectionism
- Constantly comparing yourself to others
- Feeling like you are withering instead of thriving
- Longing to "fit in" but afraid of having your "less than" secrets revealed
- Believing you aren't good enough
- Struggling to find purpose and joy in the tough times
- Wondering why you can't be more like those you admire
- Thinking you're a fraud

If any of those resonate with you, I have some great news! I have some hope to share with you. I'll share a bit of my story, some stories of others you can hear on the *Anything but Typical* podcast, and the seven weapons that I've found to be effective at silencing the imposter. Of course, your path will look different than mine and the few experiences of others we'll discuss in this book. Regardless, the weapons I've used to silence the imposter in my life can provide some hope and practical insights to set you free too.

Making this Book Work for You

- For those who want to rush to one of the most powerful of the seven weapons I've used to silence the imposter, proceed directly to the Thrive/Wither exercise in Chapter 2.

  Caution: You risk missing out on the six other effective weapons if you take this route. As effective as the Thrive/Wither exercise is, it's not a magic bullet. It's most effective when used in concert with the other six weapons.

- For those who want to dive into the seven weapons, I encourage you to read the short opening "Soccer Dad" story before diving into those seven weapons. It helps bring important context.

- I've included some highlights (and lowlights) from my anything but typical career path in case you are interested in some of the things I've learned retrospectively. For those who want to skim over most of my story and get some thought-starters for homing in on the things that make you come alive (your thrive zones) and those things that drain your battery (your wither zones), look for the **Thrive/Wither Clues** found scattered throughout my story. These were "ah-ha!" moments from my "I planned, and God laughed" journey that helped me build my own Thrive/Wither list.

- If you find personal stories interesting, I encourage you to read my story through the lens of a "contemplation springboard" to think about *your* unique story. Mine isn't nearly as important as *your* story. As you do so, please feel free to make notes about common threads in your journey. I think it will significantly help you when you decide to dive into the Thrive/Wither exercise.

Ready? Let's roll!

ACKNOWLEDGEMENTS

Long before I had heard the term "Imposter Syndrome," I was suffering from it. Even as a child, perfectionism drove me, and I felt "less than" as I compared myself to others. Those tormenting mindsets followed me into adulthood and my career for far too long.

As difficult as that can be for those suffering from imposter syndrome, it can be equally challenging for those closest to them—family, friends, and colleagues.

I can't think of anyone who has borne the brunt of these difficulties more than my wife, Jennifer. She's been by my side for over 40 years of marriage and has stuck with me through good times, disorienting moves, and a few terrifying experiences. I seriously doubt anyone else would have done that for me.

Jennifer, I can't thank you enough for your love and support for many years when I didn't know how to silence the imposter within me. I think you bore the brunt of the torment of the imposter that waged war within my mindset more than anyone. Thank you for loving me throughout all these years.

To my two sons, Josiah and Zach, thank you for loving an imperfect father who was learning on the job how to be your father from the moment when I was able to cut your umbilical cords until you left our home as young men. Next to your mother, you've had to deal with my perfectionism more than anyone else on the planet.

Thank you to my mother and deceased father for loving, nurturing, and encouraging me. Neither of you were perfectionists, nor do I believe you pushed me into it. Frankly, you frequently encouraged me to lighten up and not take life so seriously.

To the many CEOs I've been blessed to serve, coach, and know beyond the surface, thank you for humbly trusting and confiding in me. Thank you for collectively teaching me many lessons I've tried to capture in this book. Frankly, your vulnerability was the catalyst for this book.

Joe Foster, Reebok's Founder, and his wife, Jill, thank you for sharing your book writing journey and introducing me to Alicia Dunams and Authors Unite. After a year of dead ends with other publishers, I'm glad the road led me to you, Alicia, as you are the sherpa I needed! Thank you.

To Jeffrey Gitomer, Cindy Praeger, and Andy Hilliard, thank you for reading my book and your willingness to write such kind endorsements. To the brother I always prayed for but didn't meet until we became fraternity brothers in 1980, Eric Nelson, thank you for your friendship and beautiful album, "Drifting Away," that I listened to endlessly while writing this. Each of you is such a positive, ripple-making CEO with admirable accomplishments.

Finally, I want to thank Jesus, who created the heavens, the earth, and everything within them. Thank you for your creativity that's on display all around us. Thank you for making each of us "anything but typical" and proving it in the uniqueness of our fingerprints.

INTRODUCTION

Imposter Syndrome: An Abbreviated Overview

> "I have written eleven books but each time I think
> 'Uh-oh, they're going to find out now. I've run a
> game on everybody, and they're going to find me out.'"
>
> – Maya Angelou

Chances are, you've heard about imposter syndrome, have experienced it, and know even more about it than I do. If you don't, I won't bore you with its exhaustive history or rehash volumes of information and research at your command. Whether you still type your searches in various popular browsers or prefer voice command searches through tech that's available via Siri, Alexa, Google, etc., you can quickly be awash in information on this subject.

Here's a super-brief history of the term that I find interesting…

While imposter syndrome has likely been plaguing people for hundreds (if not thousands) of years, the term was first coined in the 1970s by two female psychologists who attributed this condition primarily to high-achieving women. Since then, it's become apparent that imposter syndrome isn't limited to women. Chances are, *everyone* who has walked this earth has experienced that inner voice whisper, "You're in over your head. If they only knew 'X' about you… You aren't *that* good—you've just been lucky. You've got to outwork everyone else—just to keep up. You're a fraud."

Have you ever heard any of those questions (or similar variations on those themes) rattle around in your head?

If you are honest with yourself, you likely have. But, even if you haven't, I guarantee you that you know someone who has.

One of the best visuals I've seen to illustrate one aspect of imposter syndrome is this… Imagine a circle about 1" in diameter. The words "What I know" are contained in that circle. Surrounding that little circle is a much larger circle (about 5' in diameter) with the words, "What I think others know." The reality is that we all have limited knowledge. What each of us *truly* knows is represented in that small, 1" circle versus the much larger, 5' circle. Let's face it: There will always be someone more intelligent and more knowledgeable than you; *none* of us has it all figured out. None of us is the "be-all, end-all." Each of us has something worth contributing to someone else.

Imposter syndrome, left unchecked at a minimum, can inflict unnecessary emotional suffering. Ratchet it up a notch or two, and it can sabotage meaningful relationships and/or careers. Take it to its extreme, and it can lead to debilitating depression.

Before we dive into the seven weapons that I've found to be quite effective in silencing the imposter in my head, let me clarify: I'm not a licensed mental health or medical professional. I'm just a simple dude from a little Kansas railroad town that suffered far too long in silence under the nagging whispers of imposter syndrome. I've seen these seven weapons silence it in my life. Fortunately, I've also seen them silence the imposter in the lives of others who've confided in me.

When a "Soccer Dad" Unwittingly Awakened the Imposter in Me.

"What do you do for a living?" Another soccer dad asked me on the sideline.

I wanted to lie. I was unemployed in a new city and embarrassed. Six months after moving across the country, my job vaporized. A few months later, with no income, I was living on fumes with two little boys and my wife depending on me.

I felt like a loser. As I watched my five-year-old play "swarm ball" with his little teammates, I wondered how I would provide for my young family. Honestly answering the soccer dad's question was almost too much. I paused.

"I'm unemployed." I ashamedly replied. (Lying would have only made me feel worse.)

"What's your background?" he asked.

"I've turned around and run advertising agencies," I responded.

"Send me your resume. We just re-engineered the marketing department for a large bank. They're looking for someone like you," he said.

At one of the lowest moments in my life, a complete stranger's question had the potential to dramatically change a desperate situation. I would have missed it if I had given into the pride that was tempting me to lie.

Within a few weeks, I had a job offer with a raise and a signing bonus. Crazy. Twenty years later, that soccer dad and I are still friends. I thank God for the kindness of a stranger and for the unexpected blessing of swallowing my pride.

That's a true story that happened to me 27 years before the writing of this book. But it's also an incomplete story. It didn't reveal how that soccer dad unwittingly awakened the imposter within me. *That* is what I want to address—*just in case* you need to silence the imposter too.

Besides being embarrassed about being unemployed, the imposter inside me was terrified of being exposed. It didn't want anyone to know more of the debilitating facts.

I was terrified to expose facts such as:

1. I left the agency I turned around (with my name on the door) in Kansas because I caught my business partner lying to me twice about his financial improprieties. Exposing him would have devastated him, and if I had taken the agency across the street without outing him,

I would have destroyed my name. That's why I left Wichita, KS, and moved halfway across the country to Charlotte, NC.

2. The agency I joined in Charlotte, NC, proved to be an uncalculated mistake. I brought a $2 million account and my top designer with me in exchange for equity in the firm. Once I delivered the account, finalized the slate of work, and got it approved by the client, my "partner" told me he had all he needed. My new "partner" violated our employment contract and terminated my employment. He knew I'd forgiven hundreds of thousands of dollars from my former partner. My new partner figured I wouldn't sue him for approximately $30,000 in commissions that were past due to me.

3. Of the nine months that I was in Charlotte at the time, I'd been unemployed the last three of those months when this conversation occurred on the sidelines of the soccer field.

4. I didn't want anyone to know I was a college dropout.

At the time, I felt like any one of those facts was damning and would torpedo any hope I had of getting my career out of the ditch. Too bad I hadn't yet experienced the power of the seven weapons that I've found effective in silencing the imposter...

Ready to unleash the weapons? Saddle up, my friend. Let's ride.

PART ONE

THE SEVEN
WEAPONS

CHAPTER 1

ENGAGE WEAPON #1: REALIZE THAT YOU'RE NOT ALONE

"The beauty of the imposter syndrome is you vacillate between extreme egomania and a complete feeling of: 'I'm a fraud! Oh God, they're on to me! I'm a fraud!' ..."

– Tina Fey

As mentioned in the introduction, imposter syndrome was first formally recognized and thought to be most prevalent among high-achieving women. Since then, numerous sources far more knowledgeable than me have indicated that most people walking the face of the earth have experienced it to one degree or another.

The crazy thing? Imposter syndrome can easily convince us that we're the only one that doesn't have it all together. That pesky, debilitating whisper from the imposter is such a stinking liar. The truth is that we're *not* alone and don't need to suffer in silent solitude.

Remember my opening story of the "soccer dad?" I wrote that 1,300-character post for LinkedIn 22 years *after* I experienced it. (I was terrified to hit the "post" button, but we'll cover that briefly in a later chapter.) To my great surprise, it went viral. Over eight million people read it before the algorithm slowed the reach to a crawl. It took me two hours a day, seven days a week, for four weeks to answer all the comments and direct messages I received on that post.

Eight million people responding to a post when my typical posts get a few thousand views quickly told me I wasn't alone. If you've been embarrassed to disclose something about your current situation (or past), you aren't alone. If you've ever felt like you aren't good enough, that you're in over your head, or that an aspect of your life is a fraud, I have good news: you're *not* alone!

I had a similar experience shortly after arriving in Charlotte, NC. I'd left an ad agency that had my name on the door after discovering my business partner's financial improprieties—twice. Shortly after arriving in Charlotte, a new acquaintance kept probing about what brought me halfway across the country and why I would leave my own company. As much as I didn't want to talk about what we'd experienced or how stupid I felt for having missed my partner's self-dealing that happened so blatantly under my nose, I told this new acquaintance what happened. To my surprise, he told me something similar had happened to him.

While I didn't necessarily shine a spotlight on it at that moment, I got a glimpse of how freeing it can be to realize we're not alone in most experiences. I was amazed at how fast I could move from embarrassment (and unnecessarily bound by the imposter) to experiencing a strange relief and freedom by simply bringing something I didn't want anyone to know about out of the shadows.

Have you experienced the freeing phenomenon of moving from thinking you were all alone to realizing others have had similar experiences once you had the courage to talk about it?

If so, congratulations. You've successfully engaged Weapon #1 and realized you're not alone.

If not, unsheathe this first weapon, let the light of day do its thing, and taste the freedom from isolation.

CHAPTER 2

UNLOCK WEAPON #2: DISCOVER YOUR "THRIVE/ WITHER" ZONES

"I think the most creative people veer between ambition and anxiety, self-doubt, and confidence. I definitely can relate to that. We all go through that: 'Am I doing the right thing?' 'Is this what I'm meant to be doing?'"

– Daniel Radcliffe

King Solomon, the guy credited as the wisest king to have lived, said there's "nothing new under the sun." Knowing this, I'm sure *someone* else created a version of a simple T-chart that I call the "Thrive/Wither" exercise, but before Google was a thing, I took myself through this 30-minute exercise out of necessity.

At the ripe old age of 32, it became apparent that I had to leave the company I had rebuilt from the ashes that eventually had my name on the door. I wasn't going to destroy my partner by exposing what he'd done, and I wasn't willing to ruin my reputation by taking the firm across the street while looking like I was the one who screwed my partner. Wichita, KS, is a relatively small city and, like all industries, the advertising industry was a finite fraternity of interconnected people. I had to not only leave my own company; I had to leave my city to avoid destroying either of our reputations. I needed to get *really* honest about more than my strengths and weaknesses. I needed to get introspective and honest about the things that made me come alive (thrive zones) and the things that drained my battery (wither zones). Granted, I only had 32 years of life (12 years in the full-time workforce). However, I still experienced enough work situations that gave me a limited baseline of the kinds of tasks, responsibilities, and environments that made me come alive versus those I withered.

Since my first attempt to turn intensely introspectively to do this exercise on myself, I've revisited and updated my personal Thrive/Wither T-chart annually. I usually do it between Christmas and New Year's Day when I have more time to get quiet and reflect on the past year. I also revisit it *every* time a job offer has come my way or whenever I've needed to get serious about finding a new job.

While this simple T-chart is embarrassingly simple, it's served me surprisingly well. I've also seen remarkable results with people who've reported to me, CEOs and their leadership teams that I coach, and my current employer with 80+ people. (I've included my personal Thrive/Wither responses at the end of this chapter simply for an example. The key is to follow the instructions at the end of this chapter and make the responses your own with brutal honesty.)

Whenever a company is in high-growth mode, I find that bumping up the leadership team's individual Thrive/Wither results with a simple Function Accountability Chart routinely results in massive breakthroughs for individuals on the team and the entire team. (A Function Accountability Chart is a simple listing of all the major functions in the organization and identifying who is ultimately responsible on that leadership team for each of those functions.)

Here's where the magic happens from that combo... usually, in high-growth mode, additional responsibilities get dumped on members of the leadership team. Since they are typically "good soldiers," and there's not enough cost justification yet for a new hire to address the additional workload, someone on the team sucks it up and takes it. Often, they can adequately handle the added responsibilities, but over time, they start burning out without thinking about why.

I liken this phenomenon to a boat owner wondering why their vessel is burning more fuel than usual and isn't moving as fast as it once did. Once the boat is dry docked, the owner sees the culprit—barnacles. The barnacles must get scraped off the hull before the boat can once again move more swiftly and efficiently through the water. In the same way, the responsibilities and tasks that members of the leadership team falling into their respective Wither Zones must be identified and transferred to someone else (on the leadership team or elsewhere) if they are to function at their potential and increase engagement.

A few questions for you:

1. Have you been told you were good at something but felt burned out whenever you were tasked with doing it?

2. Have you focused more on your strengths and weaknesses while failing to focus on the things that made you come alive (thrive) vs. the things that drained your battery (wither)?

3. Have you either needed to (or chosen to) make a major career change and wondered how to start?

If you've answered affirmatively to any of the above, the Thrive/Wither exercise can unlock the vault that contains the clues you need to help set you free to be uniquely you.

Before you draw your own Thrive/Wither T-chart, below is a reminder of this exercise's purpose and some basic instructions.

1. The purpose of the Thrive/Wither exercise: To identify and name the types of environments, tasks, responsibilities, etc., in which you thrive versus wither. Then, from those insights, evaluate what actions you should take.

2. Instructions: Start with the "Thrive" column and list all the types of environments, tasks, responsibilities, etc., in which you thrive—the things that make you

come alive. Then, once completed, do the same on the "Wither" side by listing the things that cause you to wither—the things that you may even be quite good at doing, yet are things that take energy from you.

Here's a sample using my Thrive/Wither responses.

Note: Don't spend more than 90-seconds reading through my answers because you must think *deeply* about your own versus taking the easy way out of copying mine—this is super important!

Thrive/Wither Exercise

Worksheet Purpose:

To identify and name the types of environments, tasks, responsibilities, etc. in which you thrive versus wither, then to evaluate what actions should be taken upon completion and review.

Instructions: Start with the "Thrive" column and list all the types of environments, tasks, responsibilities, etc. in which you thrive—the things that make you come alive. Once completed, do the same on the "Wither" side by listing things in which you wither—the things that you may even demonstrate great competency yet are things that take energy from you.

THRIVE	WITHER
• Being in charge of something	• Micro-management
• Building goal enthusiasm	• Critical, cut-throat culture
• Forging strong relationships	• No customer interaction
• Making things work	• No clearly-defined goals
• Creating & building businesses	• No learning opportunities
• Bringing a fresh perspective	• No flexibility
• Idea-generation (not paper)	• No balance
• Nimble, flexible schedule	• No upward mobility
• Selling something I believe in	• Being confined to a cube
• Contributing member of a team	• Pigeon-holed
• A learning environment	• Bureaucracy
• Limited travel (<6 nights/mo.)	• Another cog in a wheel
• Balance (exercise/health)	• Countless reports
• Longevity (can I do this at 70?)	• Gov't regulations
• Fairness & honesty	• Lack of variety
• Financial upside w/ equity	• Running operations
• Growth potential	• Stuck in details
• Forging partnerships	
• Pleasant location	
• Variety	
• Free to be myself	

THRIVE	WITHER
•	•
•	•
•	•
•	•
•	•
•	•
•	•
•	•
•	•
•	•
•	•
•	•
•	•
•	•
•	•
•	•
•	•
•	•
•	•
•	•
•	•

CHAPTER 3

IGNITE WEAPON #3:
SHINE A SPOTLIGHT ON IT

> *"To shine your brightest light is to be who you truly are."*
>
> **– Roy T. Bennett**

Of all the seven weapons I've found effective in silencing the imposter, this one takes the most courage. Yes, courage. Shining a spotlight on the very thing we don't want others to know about seems counter-intuitive and almost masochistic. I completely get it. Even so, another phenomenon that I've seen that is tied to "shining a spotlight" on the stuff we want to avoid exposing is this: doing so liberates us and often does the same for others who are captive to imposter syndrome too. What we may find embarrassing and career-limiting is rarely given much thought by others. (They're typically dealing with their imposter syndrome battles anyway!)

Here's one of my favorite examples of a very talented female CEO and business owner, Tana Greene, who did a spectacular job of shining a spotlight on her imposter syndrome in her book, *Creating a World of Difference*. Before reading her book or meeting with her in person, I knew of Tana because of her stellar reputation for being an accomplished, purpose-driven business leader with over 10,000 W-2 employees in her various companies. She was (and still is) a "Who's Who" among business leaders in my home city of Charlotte, NC. Yet, that's all I knew about her before having lunch with her years ago. At this lunch, she gave me some of her history, including shining a spotlight on some of the things that she felt like she had to hide from public view in her early career.

I encourage you to go to Amazon and buy her beautiful book for her entire story, but here are a few of the things on which she willingly shined a big ol' spotlight....

1. She got pregnant at 15 years old and gave birth to her child.
2. She married the father only to be beaten up so badly by him (as well as abandoned by him) that she wound up in the hospital.
3. Once she got out of the hospital, she returned to high school a year later and graduated as a single teenage mother—she refused to get her high school diploma via the GED.
4. She didn't get a four-year college degree—which was considered essential for most business executives then (and now).

I got to know her better once she was on the *Anything but Typical* podcast and when she invited me to coach her leadership team in one of her companies. Through these interactions, she revealed the power of shining a spotlight on the things the imposter demands to keep hidden. As a result, not only did she experience freedom, but she also helped liberate many others inspired by her incredible story.

Again, putting a spotlight on the stuff we want to keep hidden from others takes tremendous courage. However, if you are willing to be vulnerable and expose the things that your imposter demands that you keep hidden, you will massively silence that imposter in yourself, and likely help others do the same.

Are you willing to summon the courage necessary to expose what you've kept hidden to silence the imposter?

I know how scary it can be, but for your sake, I hope you can muster the courage. It will ultimately free you and likely free others.

When you do it, you'll see how this dovetails perfectly into the next weapon…

CHAPTER 4

RELEASE WEAPON #4: FOCUS ON SERVING OTHERS VS. FOCUS ON HOW THEY PERCEIVE YOU

"Imposter syndrome is an internal experience of believing you are not as competent as others perceive you to be."

– Dr. Valerie Young

I'll never forget a milestone moment in my life that burned this lesson of "focus on serving others vs. how they perceive you" into my brain.

Shortly after a private equity firm bought my consultancy, the CEO wanted to start hosting high-end "Partner Gatherings." In these gatherings, we'd get members of our 300-family investor group together, provide them updates on fund performance, give them a memorable experience that money can't buy, and facilitate meaningful connections with one another at a destination resort. One of my jobs was to orchestrate these events *and* serve as the emcee for these high-end, three-day events. The CEO was a very exacting former military officer with stringent standards and little tolerance for anything less than perfection—especially with the caliber of people we served.

The evening before I was to fly out in preparation for another big event, I was depressed. I was dreading having to emcee another event. Every word I spoke and every move I made was under the ever-critical eye of our CEO. I was always fully aware that I was in the presence of people who had been CEOs of some of the largest companies in the world and people worth hundreds of millions of dollars.

Frequently, the imposter within me was questioning, "Who am I to be in their presence, much less be the guy on stage introducing our various speakers, informing people of the various events, and making our guests feel welcome?" My imposter syndrome was hardly whispering. It seemed so loud that I figured everyone in the audience could hear it say, "Gary is in way over his head in this crowd!"

To top it off, a comment card when I was President of the dot-com publishing company seven years before this moment flooded my mind and haunted me. The comment said, "Gary's strength is in one-on-one conversations. In front of large groups? Not so much." That comment was accurate then, but it gutted me like a knife. Now, seven years later, it was cutting me again. I was repeatedly on stage for three days with a much larger, far more affluent, and discriminating audience.

The night before flying out to prep for another weeklong "partner event," I was writing in my prayer journal lamenting this situation. In my journal, I wrote out my fears, concerns, and depression to God and wondered why I was in this situation, only to be tormented in front of so many influential people. Every time I took the podium, I could easily read the audience while speaking and was hyper-sensitive when I sensed anyone was tuning me out. I imagined I felt much like Moses must have felt when his confidence was shattered after 40 years of being exiled from Egyptian royalty as a lowly shepherd. He pleaded with God to have his brother, Aaron, be his mouthpiece since Moses felt like he was "slow of speech."

During this quiet moment by myself in our basement, I don't know if it was the voice of God speaking to me or not, but this thought rang in my head with crystal-clear clarity: "A servant is not to be concerned with how they are perceived. They are to be concerned with serving. Go serve them."

My sensitivity to how others perceived me was the foundation for getting tongue-tied, stuttering, or losing my train of thought when I could sense that I wasn't resonating with the audience. I was more focused on what they thought about me than on simply serving them—regardless of what they thought of me. That week as I took the stage to welcome hundreds of our notable guests, I began my opening monologue no differently than in previous events. However, this time whenever I'd see someone who seemed to be disengaged, I'd focus my thoughts and remind myself, "Focus on serving them! How they perceive you is not to be your concern, Gary." It greatly helped.

On the last evening of the event, one of our community members (a former high-ranking executive in one of the largest food franchises in the world) came up to me and said, "Gary, I know how difficult and demanding it is to pull off events like these. I used to oversee our global franchisee events with thousands of attendees. Our standards were extremely high. But, trust me, you do it as well as anyone I've seen. You have a special way of connecting with people and making them feel welcome." I was blown away by such a compliment from such a corporate rock star. Even if her statement was grossly overinflated to be kind, it validated the importance of focusing on *serving* others versus how they might be *perceiving* me.

Asking myself this simple question in times like these gets down to the heart of the matter and helps silence the imposter: "Am I focused on serving them, or am I focused on how they perceive me?" It's a question worth asking. How we honestly answer it can make the difference between giving the imposter the microphone or silencing it.

When was the last time you dared to look at your fears and motivations to silence the imposter? Are you willing to turn your focus from what others think about you to how you can serve them?

If you can shift that focus from self to others, it's amazing how quickly you can silence the imposter.

CHAPTER 5

UNSHEATHE WEAPON #5: DIVE INTO A DAILY GRATITUDE JOURNAL

"Imposter syndrome is a thief of joy. It robs you of the ability to celebrate your achievements."

– Brené Brown

Before you tune me out on this specific weapon, hear me out. The notion of intentional gratitude and gratitude journals isn't some "kumbaya" exercise filled with incense, butterflies, and rainbows. Yeah, the Internet and social media are awash with mindset techniques and programs (many geared to grab your imagination and wallet!), but this isn't that.

Start by scratching the surface of Neuro-Linguistic Programming (NLP), and you'll quickly uncover a tight relationship between NLP and intentional gratitude. I'm *not* a psychologist, a New Age adherent, or an expert on any of those things. However, I've seen a massively positive impact in my life from the simple act of writing three journal entries in my daily gratitude journal. So, before you jump to the next chapter, it's essential to not marginalize this weapon into "I've got to get a journal, write three entries in it daily, voila! I've silenced the imposter!" It's not complicated, but it's not that simple.

First, you need to know more about my personal experience and discovery.

In 2009, my world was crashing. Within one week in June 2009, our private equity firm's bank accounts had been seized by a hostile creditor, and we were being sued for tens of millions of dollars by that creditor. Our Board of Managers ousted our CEO (someone I considered to be one of my closest friends at the time). Within a few days, we discovered much of his life within our company was a fraud. Within days, we found two outside funds that we'd invested in (including my own money and many of my friends) were Ponzi schemes. Our company didn't have the money to file for bankruptcy or pay the few of us left. We had to shut down eleven offices, address threatening lawsuits, and figure out how we could salvage any remaining assets. Investigations began. Almost daily, a new lawsuit threat came at us. Having my personal finances decimated was traumatic, but it was minuscule compared to the terrifying things that kept crashing across our bow. Just when I thought things couldn't get worse, they did. Over and over. It was like a nightmarish version of *Ground Hog Day* on perpetual repeat.

While I didn't actively contemplate suicide, I was disappointed when I awoke every morning after being frequently tormented with night terrors and panic attacks. From June until late August, at least thrice per week, I'd awaken at around 2 a.m., drenched in sweat with my heart racing at about 140 beats per minute and often feeling like someone was trying to choke me. (My resting heart rate at that time was 39.) The best word picture I can come up with was envisioning myself as a Raggedy Ann doll in the mouth of a Rottweiler being violently torn apart and shaken to the point that my stuffing was coming out and making a mess everywhere.

A concerned friend pulled me aside one day as I was walking to the office from the parking lot and said, "Frey, you don't look good. You look like you're going to die." My inner torment was showing on the outside.

In late August, I felt like my concerned friend's words were an omen. I truly felt like I was going to die. So, I called two of my closest friends in different parts of the U.S., who I've seen walk through debilitating fires of life and remain faithful men of integrity and honor. My question to each of them was the same: "I believe God's Word is true that 'perfect love casts out fear,' but I can't understand why I am so powerless against this fear when it grips me in its unrelenting stranglehold. I've memorized scriptures on fear, fasted, and prayed my guts out. Yet, it's like I have zero power over this fear."

Even though neither of my "lifeline" friends knew each other and my phone calls to each of them were separate, their responses were strangely the same. In both cases, their advice to me was, "Gary, it's about surrender. Can you trust God even if your worst fears come upon you and Jesus doesn't deliver you?"

Those tough words of wisdom shook me to my core. They confronted my misaligned, broken-record prayer that seemed to race through my mind a million times a day: "Lord, I know you *can* deliver me, but *will* You? *Please* deliver me." Repeat, repeat, repeat… Clearly, it wasn't working.

I spent the next 48 hours going down to the bedrock of everything I believed as a Christian. We had just finished a multi-month study of one of Gary Habermas' books that was an exhaustive investigation of the historical evidence of the life, death, and resurrection of Jesus purely from historical records. It was beyond compelling. My first question was, "Has God factually proven Himself throughout history beyond simply believing in the scriptures we call The Bible?" There was *far* too much historical evidence for me to discount it as belief in a nice story. The second question I asked myself was: "If someone put a gun to my head with a bullet in the chamber and said, 'Recant your faith and belief in Jesus, or I'm going to blow your brains out.' Do I have enough instances in my life that have demonstrated His reality in *my* life that I would have no option other than to say, 'I can't deny these instances in my life. Pull the trigger.'?"

After those two days of intense wrestling internally, I realized that my two wise friends' advice was my only option: *surrender* to someone who I believe is a loving, all-powerful God who doesn't owe me anything. So, while I was still amid terrifying circumstances, I changed my prayer from, "Lord, I know you *can* deliver me, but *will* You? *Please* deliver me" to "Lord, these circumstances frighten me. Even so, I surrender this situation to You. Help me to trust you even if You *don't* deliver me."

I also started seeing a pattern of how King David responded to far more frequent and far more dangerous experiences (frequently running for his very life from King Saul and even one of his treasonous sons) than I was experiencing. He didn't ignore his frightful circumstances. He often laid out his fears quite clearly and vividly, but he *always* followed his laments with two things: 1) *Remembering* God's faithfulness to him, and 2) *Giving thanks* (gratitude!). This pattern seemed to jump off the page every time I'd read through the Psalms.

So, what did I do? I started writing down a daily post on Facebook as a personal reminder and, hopefully, as an encouragement to someone else out there that began with, "It's a great day to…" followed by an encouraging scripture. I quickly amassed 391 such daily reminders.

I learned that I didn't have to be grateful *for* the terror, destruction, or genuine difficulties. However, I learned the power of finding gratitude *despite* such threats. The release seemed to rise even further when I was privileged to go through a week of intense leadership training at the BB&T Leadership Institute in 2017. While I'm forbidden to talk about the details of that transformational program, the habit of writing three journal entries in a gratitude journal massively impacted my life.

There's something so liberating and transformative from a daily practice of writing three journal entries that start with, "I'm grateful for ... " followed by a thought (usually in the form of a prayer from me to God) about that person, place, thing, observation, event, etc. that I listed. I like starting my day by journaling these entries as they seem to set the tone for the day before it starts careening down its unexpected path. I rarely skip a day, but if I do, I get back into the habit quickly because I see how tangibly it revolutionizes my perspective.

Regardless of where you are on your faith journey, I encourage you to unsheathe this mighty weapon for yourself. My advice: Find a special pen (I like using a fountain pen that was a gift from a former coaching client) and a journal that uniquely calls out your name. As of this writing, I have six years of journals that I still have in my library that no one besides me has seen. It's not for anyone else. It's for you.

I can't re-emphasize this enough. Get a special pen, a journal that you like, and start writing three entries daily in your gratitude journal, "I'm grateful for ... " followed by a thought or prayer about that specific entry. I promise you; it will change your life.

How does intentional gratitude silence the imposter? I'm not exactly sure, but it does. I think it might have something to do with this: The imposter focuses on all the things we lack. Gratitude focuses on all the blessings around us.

1. Have difficulties, imperfections, and/or life's disappointments ever consumed you to the point of despair?

2. Have you ever found that intentional gratitude didn't change your circumstances, but your attitude changed, and the despair lifted?

3. Are you inconsistent with writing down a few things for which you are grateful daily?

If so, it's time to unsheathe the fountain pen and witness the power of a gratitude journal. Once you do, you'll see how quickly the imposter is silenced.

CHAPTER 6

UNLEASH WEAPON #6: EMBRACE THE "ANYTHING BUT TYPICAL" (IN YOURSELF AND OTHERS)

"Just be you. I'll be me. And we'll meet somewhere in the middle."

– Claire Cullen

For *far* too long, I longed to fit in. I wanted to be "normal"—whatever that is. I lived under the guise that everyone else had it together, so I just needed to be like everyone else—you know, the "normal ones." (I was living in that small, 1" circle of "What I know" while envisioning that everyone else was in the gigantic, 5' circle with the words, "What everyone else knows.")

I'm ashamed that it took almost 60 years of roaming the earth to embrace the reality that we're *all* "anything but typical," as evidenced by our unique fingerprints. Think about it! Our very fingerprints testify to our uniqueness of this. Even identical twins have unique fingerprints!

As a former graphic designer, I refuse to believe this is an accident. I think it is by intentional design. As meaningless as the ads, logos, collateral, etc., were that I designed, I didn't just randomly throw words, pictures, or colors on a page and hope that something great emerged. *Everything* I designed had a purpose. *Everything* I created had intention behind it. It wasn't random. I figure that if I was that intentional about stuff with a short shelf-life with little significance in the grand scheme of life, the intricacies and uniquenesses found in nature were created with intention and by design.

Guess what? *You* are unique by design. So am I. Each of us is wired uniquely with specific perspectives and giftings. The sooner we embrace that fact, the sooner we can stop trying to be like everyone else, what someone else *thinks* we should be and comparing ourselves to others.

After all, *comparison kills gratitude.* Comparison is bondage. Think about it. There will always be someone faster, younger, stronger, smarter, wealthier, more influential, successful, etc., than you. Look at all the "influencers" on Instagram for less than 30 minutes and ask yourself, "Do I feel better about myself or worse after comparing my life with all these people?"

Gratitude is liberating. It doesn't focus on what others have that you don't. Gratitude doesn't dwell on all the areas where you've failed or how life has failed you. Instead, it finds thankfulness despite disappointments and difficulties. It finds reasons to celebrate the wonderful but often overlooked blessings of sight, breath, sound, smell, touch, and love.

Unleashing the "anything but typical" in you and embracing it in others is often the final bullet needed to silence the imposter.

That's precisely why Ben McDonald and I launched the *Anything but Typical*® podcast in January 2020. We wanted to highlight the unique stories of entrepreneurs willing to share their "behind the scenes" reel with others versus the "showreel" prevalent on Instagram, Facebook, and all the major social media platforms out there. Running a company is lonely. So often, accomplished entrepreneurs who risk everything to give flight to a dream are also unwilling subjects to imposter syndrome. You'd be surprised how many people you think have everything all together on the outside struggle with the imposter within. We aim to help everyone realize that their journey is unique and anything but typical. Even if you aren't an entrepreneur, but you enjoy hearing stories of others, I think you'll be encouraged by and learn from the often-unsung heroes we feature on this podcast. Check it out! (You can find the Anything but Typical® podcast on your favorite podcast platforms.)

Do you compare the "show reels" of others with your "behind-the-scenes" reel and feel "less-than?" If so, try embracing their uniqueness (as well as your own). You'll see gratitude grow and the imposter silently shrink.

CHAPTER 7

LAUNCH WEAPON #7: FIND SOMEONE "OUTSIDE THE JAR"

"There are an awful lot of people out there who think I'm an expert. How do these people believe all this about me? I'm so much aware of all the things I don't know."

– Dr. Margaret Chan

So far, all the weapons we've discussed rely upon *you* to do the heavy lifting of introspection, assessment, and action without spending a dime. Unfortunately, one more weapon in the arsenal can involve coughing up some money. (Don't worry, I'm not pitching you to spend any more of your hard-earned money with me besides purchasing this book.)

So, what is this ambiguous term referencing someone "outside the jar?"

Quite simply, it's often a skilled outside expert, consultant, or coach with expertise in your life that you need help in getting "unstuck" or reaching the destination you are seeking. As one of my friends says, "It's hard to read the label when you're inside the jar."

That statement is as profoundly true as it is profoundly simple.

My first experience with this notion was in 1991 with an industry expert in new business development for ad agencies. The guy who eventually became my business partner hired this new business guru at a *hefty* price of $10,000/day plus expenses—paid upfront. So why would a struggling business owner be willing to pay almost $23k/day in today's money for an outside consultant?

The answer is simple—*desperation*. My eventual business partner was losing tons of money and, frankly, didn't even have the money to go bankrupt. Hiring this well-known business development guru was a "Hail Mary" move as a last-ditch effort to save his company. The pain was excruciatingly high, so he was willing to figure out a way to pay whatever it took.

That ultimately led me into my first business turnaround at the whopping old age of 28. Part of the business development guru's solution was to hire a young buck like me, offer equity in exchange for a successful turnaround, and implement some of his strategies for growing the business. (Chapter 10 dives into much more of the details surrounding this.)

The guru was well-known and respected in our industry, and he had no qualms about charging handsomely for his services.

My eventual business partner had to pay the first round of fees. Still, after I joined the firm and became an equity partner, I shared the financial sacrifice for coughing up the money to pay the business development guru's pricey fees. Repeatedly, I had to dig deep into contemplating the risk/reward for returning this guru to Wichita, KS. As much as those financial sacrifices stung, having a competent expert "outside the jar" paid off in spades. I learned that with each sacrificial payment, we were making a calculated investment in our growth. It *always* paid off. Always.

Here's the fascinating thing: *rarely* did the guru tell us something we didn't already know. However, his insights gave us the courage and confidence to take decisive action. He could help us read the label because he was outside the jar of our "inside the jar" perspectives, fears, and biases.

Years later, when I was coaching CEOs full-time, I did a humorous little sixty-second video about why a pro golfer like Tiger Woods would hire a swing coach who couldn't hold a candle to him on the course. It was about the objectivity of a qualified, outside perspective—having someone "outside the jar" to help read the label. Coincidentally, the PGA Championship was in town then, and a notable player in that tournament was sitting beside me in our local YMCA locker room. It was during the week of the practice round for the tournament, and we struck up a conversation. After I got past the embarrassment of not recognizing this famous pro golfer (I suck at golf, so I don't play golf nor follow it), I told him about this video I'd posted on LinkedIn. He asked to see it. I played it for him; he laughed and told me that I nailed it.

Have you ever felt "stuck" when trying to solve a problem or tormented by a debilitating mindset only to have someone "outside the jar" help liberate you with a perspective you hadn't seriously considered? If so, you've experienced the impact from launching the seventh weapon.

If not, invest in yourself. Find someone "outside your jar" to help you read the label and silence the imposter.

Storyline bonus: A few days after this exchange with the famous pro golfer (still during the practice round), I was sitting outside with a friend at my favorite local coffee shop near the country club hosting the PGA tournament. The pro golfer and his caddy walked past my friend and me, then the pro golfer stopped, turned around, and said to me, "Hey, mate! I didn't recognize you with your clothes on!" He then proceeded to go into the coffee shop without missing a beat. (Remember, we met in the YMCA locker room a few days before this.)

My friend sitting with me happened to be a good golfer and massive golf enthusiast. (He also knew how bad of a golfer I was.) He stared at me in amazement and said, "How do you know *him*?" Needless to say, both my friend and I will never forget that moment or how validating the pro golfer was for the importance of having someone "outside the jar" to help us read the label if we're going to see growth in areas that are important to us—including silencing the imposter.

*   *   *

Now, you know the seven weapons for silencing the imposter. Unfortunately, they won't do anything to silence the imposter by themselves. You must take action, dust them off, and deploy them. I hope they will be as effective for you in silencing that nasty imposter as they have been for me.

If you want to read about more of my crazy journey and see the patterns that unfolded in helping me discover the stuff in my own thrive and wither zones, read on. Again, what I've written about in upcoming chapters should be approached from the perspective of your quest for what makes you come alive or drains your battery, rather than just my own story. That's where the power for your transformation resides.

If you aren't interested in my "I planned, and God laughed" journey and want to focus on deploying the seven weapons I've outlined previously, thank you for your time. I hope these weapons help you (or someone you love) effectively silence that nasty, lying, and tormenting imposter.

PART TWO

UNCOVERING "THRIVE/ WITHER CLUES" IN AN "ANYTHING BUT TYPICAL" JOURNEY

CHAPTER 8

PRAYING FOR "NORMAL" WHEN IT'S JUST A SETTING ON THE DRYER

"Today, I feel much like I did when I came to Harvard Yard as a freshman in 1999 ... I felt like there had been some mistake—that I wasn't smart enough to be in this company and that every time I opened my mouth, I would have to prove I wasn't just a dumb actress ..."

– Natalie Portman

As far back as I can remember, I prayed for a "normal" life. I don't know if it was the stares of other people as I walked alongside my father as he limped, dragging his right leg that was stricken by polio when he was only 17. I don't know if it was the fact that my parents were a bit older than the parents of other kids my age. I don't know if it was the fact that I was routinely the last kid chosen to be on a variety of teams.

I know that praying that my family and I would simply be "normal" was a regular thing even as a young child once I was tucked into bed and the lights went out.

Don't get me wrong; I think I had a great childhood. What you are about to read isn't a sob story as I was truly blessed. What you are about to read is what I think might be the framework for my belief that "normal" is something we should strive for and attain.

That silly, idealistic boy became a silly, idealistic man who kept chasing the grand illusion of "normal" for decades.

Growing up as a kid, we had many kids in our blue-collar neighborhood in our small Kansas railroad town of 16,000 people surrounded by farm communities. We played outside until our mothers called us in for dinner, then back to an intense "kick the can" game until it got dark. We rode our bikes with playing cards making a pseudo-motorized sound held in place by clothespins on the frame attached to the back wheel and up plywood ramps to help us pretend we were riding motorcycles like Evel Knievel.

We didn't watch much T.V. besides the staples of "Hee Haw," "I Love Lucy," "The Carol Burnett Show," and "The Lawrence Welk Show." Once I got old enough to be my dad's "helper"— the fetcher of tools and holder of things since my dad couldn't move fast with only one leg, cartoons on Saturday morning were severely limited. Heck, with only three channels plus PBS (the channel my little sister liked because of Sesame Street) in fuzzy black and white, T.V. wasn't as addictive as all the addictive electronic attention-suckers we have available today, vying for our time.

Even with limited T.V. watching, those darn commercials indicated that "normal" was out there. It just wasn't at our house. Name brand clothes? My mom made a lot of ours. Name brand shoes? We bought off-brand shoes because they were what we could afford. I remember being in 7th or 8th grade before I got my first pair of Converse All-Stars for playing basketball. For a moment, those Converse made me think I just might have a shot at "normal."

Thrive/Wither Clue: What the media or others try to convince us is "normal" isn't necessarily so. I "wither" when I feel like I'm supposed to conform to the norm.

Being raised in the strike zone of "Tornado Alley" in the middle of Kansas, having a basement was "normal." Unfortunately, our house didn't have one, so we had to run to our neighbors in the middle of pouring rain and wind whenever those terrifying tornado sirens would suddenly blare—often at night. We eventually had a basement dug under our existing house when I was around 10 or 11. Thank you, Lord, for progress towards "normal!"

Playing baseball in the summer is a "normal" pastime in the U.S. As a grade-schooler, I wanted to play with my friends as it was what everyone else did—at least the ones I considered to be "normal." Unfortunately, those blistering hot summer

Kansas days and evenings combined with itchy, heat-trapping uniforms and my *zero* talent for the game didn't work out so well. My coach relegated me to right field, and I'm confident that my coach must have prayed that the center fielder could run fast to cover right field for me in case the ball got hit into my assigned area of the outfield. I couldn't catch worth a darn, couldn't throw the ball where I wanted it to go, and couldn't hit. Other than that, I was a great baseball player! After every game, I was so stressed out about being embarrassed by my abysmal abilities at these games that I developed a massive headache. (We now know them as migraines.) The cold Shasta soda after the game was the only thing I could look forward to before I would get ushered to bed long before it was bedtime.

When I was in middle school, kids teased me by being called "Mr. Perfect." It wasn't that I was perfect—not by a long shot. It was because I idealistically thought the false realities promoted by T.V. ads and movies were attainable—more "normal" than what I was experiencing. The more I tried to be perfect, the more kids teased me, and the more inferior I felt.

It was in middle school that I learned about short-term and long-term goals. There, I put those lessons to work by learning to ride a unicycle. I figured if I couldn't fit in by being like everyone else, I'd try to do something not everyone else could. I had swollen, black and blue ankles from all my failed attempts, but I got the hang of it little by little.

It was also about this time when I *finally* convinced my mom to let me quit piano lessons. (I didn't like how practicing prevented me from playing outside with my neighborhood friends.) Eventually, she let me attempt something I *really* wanted to learn: drums. Something about being a rock drummer grabbed me. Drummers had all the cool gear, sat on a throne, and were an essential part of a greater collective—a band. Once I got my first drum kit, I couldn't stop practicing. I loved everything about being a drummer—the music, playing loud, being uninhibited while hiding behind the drum kit, and most importantly, being part of a band.

I got to hear Buddy Rich perform live at a band competition, and while you might think that was an out-of-body experience, something bigger hit me. As much as I love hearing great drummers, I can only handle a few minutes of drum solos. I can listen to great bands for *hours,* but I can only stand a few minutes of great drum solos. Why? I think drums are heartbeat instruments that function at their best as part of an ensemble—not solo instruments.

Thrive/Wither Clue: I "thrive" when I'm in charge of something (like keeping time) while being part of a bigger group.

As much as my desire to "fit in" was somewhat met by being in a band throughout high school, into college and for decades after college, my thoughts routinely tormented me by insisting I wasn't "good enough." I constantly compared myself to the best drummers in the world playing in my favorite bands. Yet, I always fell short of my ideals—no matter how hard I practiced or how many lessons I continued to take.

Before I was legally old enough to drive, I was driving tractors in the field in the summer for my grandpa's dairy and wheat farm. I started with a small, old Ferguson tractor to rake hay into windrows in preparation for bailing. Then, I quickly "graduated" to plowing fields with one of my grandpa's much larger, more powerful "big boy" John Deere 4020 tractors. Even though I wasn't yet in high school, I somehow felt "manly" after a long, lonely day on a tractor without an enclosed cab when I'd realize how sweaty and dirty I was once I hit the shower late at night.

One thing about it, driving a tractor all day is a *lonely* experience. I remember thinking, "I miss being around my friends out here."

Thrive/Wither Clue: I like working hard and seeing results, but I "wither" in long expanses of time of solitude.

My cousin, who was also my age, also worked the fields of our grandpa's farm. The primary difference was I was a "town kid," and he was a "farm kid," as his family farm was just down the road from my grandpa's farm. I don't think my grandpa treated us differently, but for some reason, I felt like "less than" my cousin when we were around my grandpa. They had more stuff in common. I wasn't a *real* farm kid. I felt like an imposter.

Have you ever felt that way? Isn't it crazy how "imposter syndrome" can be sensed—even as a kid?

Thrive/Wither Clue: Comparison is a cruel taskmaster and can take us away from finding joy in our uniqueness. Comparing myself to others makes me "wither."

An unlikely place where I seemed to find a place of belonging and normalcy was in the swimming pool. Unlikely? Well, considering I flunked beginners swimming lessons when I was five or six years old, coupled with the fact that the varsity swim coach was the same woman who failed me a decade earlier, yes, unlikely.

When I heard that our high school was starting a co-ed varsity swim team, a couple of my equally unathletically inclined friends and I thought the swim team would be an easy ticket to a coveted letter jacket. Instead, we had a rude awakening. I almost quit during the first week of two-a-day practices. I hated getting up early and diving into a cold pool during those dark and freezing-cold Kansas winter mornings. Feeling like I was going to drown at each practice made it worse. Had it not been for my father's persistent encouragement to stick it out, I would have quit.

Swimming is a challenging and lonely sport. However, I had a few things motivating me: 1) I wanted to "fit" in via some athletic sport (and be a four-year letterman); 2) My fragile self-esteem couldn't bear being beaten by a girl (the other butterflier on the team was a girl who went on to become an All-American swimmer in college), so I had to work hard; 3) I wanted to win more for my fellow relay team members than I even wanted to win an individual event.

Thrive/Wither Clue: I swam my fastest splits on the relays because I love winning as a contributing team member more than I love winning by myself. I "thrive" when I'm a member of a high-performing team.

After my first-year season, I earned that coveted varsity swimming letter jacket. However, it didn't quench my thirst to be "normal" and fit in. Without going into all the details, I didn't just wade into drinking alcohol; I dove into the deep end before my freshman year was over. It seemed like everyone was doing it. After all, that is what "normal" looked like in the mid-1970s, right?

Like other teenagers who made foolish choices doing stupid things, we had more than our share of near misses with disaster and even death. While it was fun for a season, I was racked with guilt every night I'd come home, lie to my parents, have bed-spins, and ask God to forgive me—knowing full well I'd be right back on the same self-destructive road as soon as the following weekend rolled around.

As a freshman varsity letterman and going to keg parties, I seemed to be "fitting in" with the crowd. But, inside, I knew I still didn't fit. Besides, I wasn't a funny drunk. Once I hit the tipping point, I got sad and cried.

Fortunately, that season of my life didn't last that long. I had a geometry teacher that saw what was happening to many of us. He stopped class one day during my sophomore year and challenged us to consider the potential outcomes of the paths we were pursuing. It had nothing to do with geometry. It had everything to do with spirituality. He was one of the sponsors of the Fellowship of Christian Athletes (FCA), and that classroom wake-up call was a gutsy move for a public educator.

While I didn't make any significant moves that school year, his words and challenge continued to ring inside my head. Going along with the crowd and doing what "normal" teenagers were doing wasn't satisfying. Something had to give. I don't remember the exact moment or day, but I remember deciding to quit drinking and start pursuing God on His terms to the best of my ability. My friends didn't really get it, but they still allowed me to hang out with them. "Mr. Perfect" didn't walk out his Christian faith perfectly, but for some reason, this "faith thing" felt right even though I was consciously choosing not to partake in "normal" teenage behaviors.

Thrive/Wither Clue: What may be "normal" for others can lead us furthest away from what makes us come alive. Trying to be "perfect" makes me "wither."

By my senior year in high school, I had shown some promise in art, and I needed to start thinking about college. I didn't have a clue about what I could do with art other than being an art teacher, and that didn't sound that appealing to me. One of our close family friends was an accomplished architect in town. His oldest son swam with me on our high school swim team, and I thought their family was the ideal family. He had a "Brady Bunch" modern house, a swimming pool, and three kids (all were close to my age). He was fun to be around and cool. He thought architecture would be a good fit for me. He gave me a massive head start on architecture school by asking me to be an apprentice for his architecture firm for a couple of hours a day. I loved him, his family, and his encouragement.

I enrolled in one of the top architecture programs in the U.S.: Kansas State University—the same place where my architecture mentor graduated. Fortunately, my apprenticeship gave me an unfair advantage over my classmates during my freshman year at KSU. My favorite professor was a practicing architect in New York City on a teaching sabbatical at KSU. After our first semester's final project, he pulled me aside and told me he wanted me to work for him in New York. It terrified me. I'd never been to a massive city like New York, and I was intimidated.

I also realized that architecture had long project times (much longer than my short attention span liked) and required lots of model building. (I sucked at building models.) So, while I loved the design aspects of architecture, I came to grips with the fact that I was pursuing architecture more out of my admiration for my architect mentor than for the love of designing buildings.

Thrive/Wither Clue: I began learning that the stuff that made great architects made me "wither."

I switched majors from architecture to graphic design and advertising. Much shorter project times, no model building, and seemingly more creative freedom seemed to suit me better. In addition, the design department head was another professor with much real-world experience versus many professors whose career was only in academia. She quickly became my favorite professor; she genuinely wanted me to succeed. She recommended I find a summer internship with a graphic design firm after my sophomore year.

Fortunately, I got lucky and landed a summer internship with a small design firm headed by a talented designer. I worked for the design firm in the mornings, managed our town's municipal swimming pool in the afternoons, worked the closing shift at my dad's family video arcade a few nights a week, and volunteered at a Christian "coffee house" for high schoolers a couple of nights a week.

Thrive/Wither Clue: I "thrive" on variety and being around different groups of people.

The plans that I had got thrown a curve ball that summer. While I was not interested in dating that summer, I met a girl at the coffee house who rocked my world. I fell madly in love with her, and before summer was over, we both knew we wanted to marry each other. One of the challenges: I planned to return to Kansas State University while she planned to attend a local, private, two-year college, Hesston College. Another challenge was I was only 20 years old, and she was only 18.

To complicate things further, the design firm where I'd completed my internship offered me a full-time job. When I had to present my portfolio of work from my summer design internship to my advisor back at Kansas State, she gave me advice that rocked my parents (both college grads) and fueled my inner insecurities. After reviewing my portfolio, she said, "It's clear you have been working under a talented designer. In all my years of teaching, I've never given this advice to anyone else, but I think you should take the job. Unfortunately, we are at the highest levels of unemployment since the Great Depression, and graduates aren't finding jobs." (That was in 1982.)

I was a Putnam Scholar at KSU. That academic scholarship paid for 100% of my tuition. Unfortunately, dropping out meant that I couldn't get it back, should I attempt to return to KSU sometime in the future.

Not only would I be dropping out of college for a job that paid $10,500/year with no benefits, but I was also going to get married a year later. That certainly didn't appear to be "normal."

Thrive/Wither Clue: Failing to follow a traditional path doesn't have to mean failure. Linear courses are theoretical and unnatural. Curves and meanderings abound in nature. I "thrive" in non-traditional paths.

CHAPTER 9

HIDING BEHIND A MUSTACHE—DEALING WITH IMPOSTER SYNDROME

"Every time I was called on in class, I was sure that I was about to embarrass myself. Every time I took a test, I was sure it had gone badly. And every time I didn't embarrass myself—or even excelled—I believed that I had fooled everyone yet again. One day soon, the jig would be up..."

– Sheryl Sandberg

You must remember that in 1982, "Magnum P.I." and Tom Selleck's signature mustache were in vogue. Growing my version of that signature 'stache was my way of trying to look less like a 20-year-old college dropout but more of an adult working in the "real world" as a graphic designer. I have some hilarious photos trying to look older than I was with my formidable mustache.

Without realizing it, I was a year away from getting married, but I was already nurturing "imposter syndrome"—a cruel inner torment of feeling "less than" others. I was convinced that everyone but myself knew what they were doing, but if they only knew how incapable I was, I was sure they'd reject me.

So, hiding behind my mustache of insecurity, I did what I thought I should do—I tried to outwork everyone else and push myself hard in any area that garnered me any kind of respect or praise.

By day, I learned everything I could under the talented founder of the design studio that hired me after my internship. By night, I worked at my father's family arcade a few nights a week as I continued to volunteer at the Christian coffee house and played drums for my uncle's fledgling church. With all my "free time," I spent as much time as possible with my beautiful, young fiancée while she was in her first year of college. As packed as my schedule was, I had a blast that year.

A few months before getting married in 1983, I applied for a job that was a 45-minute drive away because I needed something that the design studio didn't provide: benefits. It was the first of only *two* advertised positions I applied for and landed in my entire career. My new boss told me that over 100 people submitted applications for that job that paid $11,500 annually (plus health insurance). To my great surprise, I was the one they chose.

I worked an early shift as a designer at this firm that specialized in vinyl graphics for everything from motorcycle helmets to motorhomes. My first design project was for a special edition of a Jeep CJ7. As a non-morning person, I didn't enjoy getting up so early, but the early start time afforded me time in the afternoon to moonlight for a few more hours each day for the design firm I'd left.

The sales team at the vinyl graphics firm loved having me work on their projects that they pitched to all the major boat and R.V. manufacturers. They told me that my work was easy to sell to prospects. Their encouragement seemed to propel my creativity levels and fueled my drive.

Thrive/Wither Clue: That sense of winning as a team and some positive affirmation makes me "thrive."

After a year of working both jobs, the original design firm that hired me after my internship offered me more money and benefits to rejoin them full-time. The thought of not having to get up so early to make that 45-minute drive each day to the vinyl graphics firm *plus* more money sounded *fantastic* to me, so I leaped at their offer.

As time progressed, things started changing. My boss/mentor seemingly began turning every project into a competition. I certainly didn't see myself as a threat, but on a couple of projects that both of us submitted designs to the clients, my designs got selected. Critical, condescending comments started coming my way, cloaked as jokes. The problem was they didn't feel like jokes. They stung.

Thrive/Wither Clue: Being in a cut-throat, critical, and non-team-oriented culture makes me "wither."

I didn't think I was good enough to work in a larger market with more sophisticated design firms, so I resigned myself to gutting it out. Before long, the design firm had cash flow problems, and our office manager would alert me whenever there were insufficient funds to cover my paycheck. She told me to get cash from the firm's bank via their drive-thru lane as she knew we were living paycheck to paycheck. (For some reason, she felt the drive-thru lane would give me a better chance of converting my check into cash than if I went in. Whether her theory was true or not, I got that precious cash for my paycheck each time I followed her instructions.)

Again, to my surprise, my second attempt at getting hired from an ad worked. I got called for an interview with a portfolio review, and it landed me a job with one of the most respected design firms in the state. I was the youngest designer to be named art director at this prestigious firm. I was also the only one on that team without a college degree. The founder was a bit of a legend in town, as he had done some of the original design work for Pizza Hut when he was about my age. He was about 30 years older than I was and became my first real professional mentor as an adult. He taught me so much about trusting my gut, finding joy in exceptional design, and pushing the creative envelope by trying solutions others were afraid to attempt. He also taught me never to apologize for charging more than the competition when you deliver a higher level of service and a better product.

One of my favorite experiences was when we were competing against one of the world's largest ad agencies based in Chicago for a prestigious new project that Cessna Aircraft was launching. Our firm was like David versus Goliath, but we were united in our resolve and enthusiasm. Our firm submitted over 60 different logos for this shoot-out against the big Chicago agency. (That certainly was a case of overkill as I look back on it now.) Cessna picked three logos as their finalists. All three were mine, and they ultimately selected my favorite one. This prestigious event temporarily buoyed my self-esteem despite my youth and lack of a degree.

I was one of only a few of the art directors who also managed the firm's key clients. That meant I was responsible for working directly with marketing directors and CEOs, managing profit and loss for the work, etc. I discovered I loved building relationships with clients and bridging the gap between typical, right-brained "creative types" and left-brained "business types."

Thrive/Wither Clue: As much as I loved designing, I also loved forging long-term relationships based on solving problems in a manner that is in the client's best interest.

Shortly after, our founder and his wife decided that Scottsdale, AZ, would be a great market to move our headquarters to, and they wanted me to be part of the launch team. So, the founder flew my wife and me, plus our infant son, to Scottsdale to go house hunting. Unexpectedly, neither of us could get comfortable moving so far away from our families. It was difficult for me to tell my boss this news. He was such an excellent mentor, and I knew it would disappoint him. After breaking the news to him, I knew I would need to find another job since his focus was clearly on building the Scottsdale office.

One of the largest ad agencies in the state knew about our design firm's plans to relocate to Scottsdale, and the founder asked me to meet with him at the fanciest club in the city. They wanted me to join them as an art director. I was honored. I'd never been to such a fancy restaurant. During the discussion, I asked about my level of client interaction. The founder surprised me with his response of, "little to none." As an art director, I would work on high-profile T.V. spots and print ads, but the account service team handled all client interactions. As much as I wanted validation from being hired by this big firm and working on highly prized T.V. spots, I knew I wouldn't be happy without having some client interaction.

Thrive/Wither Clue: I "thrive" when I'm interacting with clients, and not being relegated to the creative barracks.

Thanks to an intro from some of my friends who left local T.V. stations as journalists, one of the co-founders of a video production company liked my creative eye. They hired me as they thought my addition could strengthen their foothold with one of their largest clients—one of the largest privately held companies in the world. Unfortunately, it was also a big client of my prior mentor who had relocated to Scottsdale, AZ. So, unintentionally, I found myself in a fight for a massive, high-profile project for this prestigious client between my mentor and my new employer. During the shoot-out, I found out that my mentor sent a note to the client acknowledging my talent but with this caveat: "…for someone without a college degree."

Ouch. Hearing that from my mentor hit me straight in my heart. My greatest sense of vulnerability and shame had just been called out to the open by a mentor I deeply respected and loved. My imposter syndrome was awakened with a vengeance. I was exposed. Even though my mentor acknowledged my gift as a designer, I couldn't receive any of that. All I could do was focus on the asterisk: "for someone without a college degree."

The client forced both of our companies to share the project. I loved working on the project, and the final product was beautiful. The collaboration worked, but I couldn't shake how my mentor had unintentionally thrown salt in my open wound.

After a summer of flying around the country on several of the client's private aircraft shooting still photos and video for this project, I started spending all my time at the video production studio. One of the co-founders loved teaching me 3-D animation and took me under his wing. Unfortunately, the other co-founder had a quiet, self-righteous demeanor that seemed to oppress the entire staff. He was proud of our Mission Statement that was so broadly and proudly emblazoned on the wall of our reception area. Unfortunately, he was oblivious that his actions undermined every word of that mission statement.

It was initially subtle, but I could see once-confident videographers and writers withering. Before long, it made its way to my office as well. Soon, I *dreaded* Mondays. The dread started on Sunday night; without exception, I started having debilitating migraines *every* Monday. I could barely make the 45-minute drive home by channeling airflow to my forehead with my sunroof open. Once home, I asked Jennifer to keep our little boys at bay as I made my way up to our bedroom, locking the door, shutting the blinds, and sleeping for a couple of hours before I felt well enough to go downstairs and get some protein in me.

The quality of my work started to slip. I thought I must have oversold my abilities. I started feeling like I was lucky to have someone like the critical co-founder bestow mercy on me and provide me with a job. He knew I was a college dropout and reminded me that a college dropout like me was lucky to be working at such a place. My self-esteem that once soared was subterranean.

Thrive/Wither Clue: Micro-managing, critical bosses can affect our health if we let them. I "wither" under micromanagement.

BONUS Thrive/Wither Clue: Lofty Mission Statements not upheld by actions create cynics within the organization. Words must be backed up with action. I "thrive" when mission statements are backed up with actions in a culture.

One day of fate, a friend stopped by our offices to drop something off for one of our video producers. He stopped by my office and told me the latest industry gossip in the city: *The* hottest, most award-winning ad agency in town was looking for a senior art director. He thought I should throw my hat into the ring. Even though I had *zero* confidence in my abilities at that point and felt destined to stay in the crucible of criticism (so I could have my character refined, evidently), I called my wife to tell her this news. She saw what was happening to me and said, "As soon as we hang up, you call them and tell them you want to be in the consideration set. Once you've made the call, please call me to confirm you did it." I thank God for this woman. This instance is one of a handful of times she likely saved my life.

Again, to my surprise, I was invited to apply for the job via an interview and portfolio review. In addition, this potential employer hit me with something I'd never experienced at this point in my career: three "spec creative" projects to see how I would address three vastly different types of real-world creative challenges. They included an honor-system requirement that limited my time to 1.5 hours per project. We met just before a three-day holiday weekend. They wanted to meet with me early the next week and review my three projects.

Though tempted to spend more time on these projects than the 1.5-hour limit, I honored their request. I convinced myself that all my projects *sucked*. Frankly, I was embarrassed with my results; I thought my imposter syndrome would be exposed again. I didn't want to present my work, but I'd made a commitment to show up, so I went back for what I was sure would be a meeting of humiliation.

They *liked* my thinking. What? I was blown away. They designed their test projects to expose the finalists' thought processes and integrity. It would have been apparent if I had spent more time spit-polishing my three projects. They hired me on the spot.

It still blows me away how quickly I returned to a place of thriving at work after feeling like I was dying each day at my previous employer. I was almost instantly producing my most creative work. I was part of a fun, talented, competitive, team-oriented culture that made me come alive.

Thrive/Wither Clue: I "thrive" when I'm accepted for who I am and I'm free to be a contributing part of a high-performance team.

CHAPTER 10

THE MUSTACHE IS GONE, BUT THE INSECURITY IS STILL HIDING BENEATH THE SURFACE

"Imposter syndrome is a feeling that you have given everyone the wrong impression, that you are not as talented as they think you are."

– Seth Godin

As my confidence grew, the need to hide behind my walrus mustache subsided, so I shaved it and opted for a trendy cross between a mullet and a perm. (I'll never know how we thought that look was good!) I felt I finally found a place where I belonged.

Unfortunately, my dream gig was far too short-lived. In less than two years, another agency acquired our creative hot shop—primarily for one of our large national clients. All members of our all-star creative team were soon to be unemployed.

We found out on December 7—the same day as the Japanese attack on Pearl Harbor decades earlier. I called my wife and told her the shocking news. I asked her to take back all her recently purchased Christmas presents. Our meager bank account was also under attack with two weeks' warning and no severance. (Ironically, the ad agency that bought us was the same agency that tried to hire me as an art director years before.)

Since my wife was busy as a stay-at-home mom to our two boys, who were both under four years old, I had to scramble. I reached out to every design firm and ad agency contact I had to drum up whatever freelance work I could find. Fortunately, the floodgates opened. I said "yes" to every project someone offered and worked crazy hours to complete the work. I was blessed financially, but the lack of sleep (partly with a newborn in the house), stress from lack of health insurance beyond December, and being a solo act wore me out.

Shortly after the new year began, a stranger called me out of the blue. That call unexpectedly and quickly changed my life. He was a well-known, highly compensated "rainmaker" that ad agencies worldwide used to help them grow their companies. A local ad agency owner hired him as a "Hail Mary" move as a last-ditch effort to save his agency from going bankrupt. The rainmaker had asked around the city for a young, talented designer who might be interested in an equity offer and their "name on the door" in return for helping them turn the agency around to profitability. My name repeatedly came up as I had recently made the rounds looking for freelance work, and my name was top-of-mind for many.

Even though I needed a job with benefits and wanted to be part of a team, I was a college dropout with no experience in turnarounds; I was sure I wasn't a fit. I told the rainmaker guru that at only 28 years old, I didn't think I was the person he was seeking. He pushed back and said I was the right person for this job because his client wanted to occupy the "creative hot shop" position that my former ad agency had occupied before they got gobbled up by one of the city's largest agencies. All the data points he listed resonated with me as I had first-hand experience in the things he outlined.

Thrive/Wither Clue: Even if we don't have all the experience or expertise a role requires, we might be surprised to find we fit when we consider the primary qualities needed and our ability to deliver. I "thrive" when I focus on what I have to offer vs. what I don't.

After meeting with the business growth guru and his client, who was 20 years older than me, I agreed to take the job. I believed I could help the agency eventually claim that "creative hot shop" position in the market. However, I had one condition: I didn't want equity or my name on the door since I was actively trying to get my young family to the South, closer to some of my wife's family. Plus, I wanted to be in a bigger ad agency market. (I was interviewing at Coca-Cola, and I desperately thought that if I could get hired by such an iconic brand, I could silence that "You're just a college dropout" voice in my head.) Finally, I thought that while it might take some time to go through the bureaucratic hiring process for Coke, this would be a short-term gig that would help the agency owner and provide me with some steady income.

Within a few weeks, we had some good news and bad news. The good news? We beat out two of the largest agencies in the city in a pitch for a big bank client. The bad news? We came in second place to the largest agency in the state. Second place pays the same as the last place: *zero*. Our firm was hemorrhaging money, so we immediately had to take 20% pay cuts to slow the bleeding. Before long, everyone quit except for me, my "partner," and his part-time assistant.

That forced me to handle almost everything outside of my partner's public relations (PR) expertise. I became the designer, writer, biller, and seller of all our creative products (ads, brochures, direct mail, TV, etc.) outside of PR. I changed how we estimated and billed for our work as well. We were profitable in less than a year and, to our surprise, we turned heads at the local creative awards show.

Even though nothing was moving on the job I was chasing with Coca-Cola, I still was set on landing a job in the South. I told my partner that he needed to replace me with three people: an account service person (sales), a copywriter, and a digital designer to get us into the digital age. The challenge: we didn't have much money to spend on three new salaries. We had to get *really* creative.

Fortunately, one of my colleagues at the creative hot-shop agency, who also lost his job on December 7 a couple of years prior, was teaching creative advertising courses at the local state university. He knew all the undiscovered creative and driven students. He led me to our creative copywriter and digital designer. I called one of my best friends (the bass player from my college band) who was still working for the video production company, as I knew he wasn't happy there. I was confident he could be a great account executive and help us with his formidable journalism skills. We made three *outstanding* hires.

Thrive/Wither Clue: Building and maintaining long-term relationships matters to me. They transcend company affiliations and geographies. I "thrive" when I'm allowed to do so.

My focus on finding something back in the South was waning. I was too busy having fun in this "short-term" gig. We were winning business. My family was happy. I decided moving to the South wasn't worth losing what we were building in Kansas. I asked my partner to honor his original equity offer with my name on the door. He jumped at the idea. We changed the agency's name to include my name on it, and I took my equity in the form of phantom stock. (That proved to be a wise move. I'll explain in a bit.)

We kept doing well at the awards shows, getting work published in prestigious industry publications, and winning big pieces of business. Then, we bought and renovated an old chili factory in the part of the city that was at the forefront of a massive revitalization. I thought I was in my "forever" career home.

We had secured all the North American business for our largest client, an international aircraft manufacturer, but I wanted the rest of their international business. The client wanted us to win it too, but we needed a European presence to secure that piece of their business. So, we called the business growth guru originally responsible for getting me placed here for guidance.

He sent his mergers and acquisitions (M&A) expert to spend a day with us and give us his recommendation. As he reviewed our financials, he was impressed by our company's dramatic turnaround over the past few years. The only thing he thought was out of line was the amount of money we were spending on outside consultants. Given his boss' day rate of $10k/day plus travel expenses, he figured we'd had his boss (the business growth guru) visit us a lot that year.

I knew his boss hadn't been engaged that year by us and when I saw the six-figure amount in that line item, my heart sank. I asked my partner what was in the "consultants—other" line item. He got red-faced, and beads of sweat started forming on his brow. He stated he would need to check into it and quickly changed the subject. The M&A expert didn't know he'd just uncovered my partner's massive betrayal or his extensive financial improprieties. I can't convey the hurt and betrayal I felt towards this partner of mine, who was as much a father figure to me as anything.

Without going into the depth and pain of the betrayal, I caught, confirmed, and confronted my partner's malfeasance—twice. I knew I had a choice to make. Either I exposed his deeds to the world, which would have destroyed him and his name. Or I took the firm—filled with all the coworkers I hired and loved—across the street and ruined my name unless I was willing to destroy him by exposing what he'd done. I was in a lose/lose situation. I wasn't ready *or* willing to do either option.

Thrive/Wither Clue: Relationships based on trust and integrity are much more valuable to me than any amount of financial wealth. I "wither" when trust is broken, and integrity is lacking.

(Believe me, there's another book's worth of material just from that nightmarish scenario, but we'll leave that for another day.)

Since I wasn't willing to destroy my partner by exposing his misdeeds (nor was I keen on muddying my name as it would appear as though I stole my firm from my partner if I didn't "out" him), I knew I had to leave my own company and my city. So, I called my most significant mentor, who split time between Minneapolis and New York. I told him what I'd discovered, how I'd first confronted my partner, and that I'd caught him again. Then, I asked for his advice. He suggested I move to the best market for advertising—New York City.

As much as I wanted to be in the same city as my favorite mentor and where the big brands and big budgets roamed, I simply couldn't see taking my wife and two young children to New York. My career was important to me, but my family's well-being was even more so. We had no family near New York, and the thought of moving from a town of a few hundred thousand people to a city of eight million was too much for us to consider.

Thrive/Wither Clue: Location for my career matters to me. I need a place that is also a healthy place for my family.

My second call was to the business growth guru and his M&A expert. They knew me, our success, and they unwittingly stumbled upon the life-changing revelation. Every ad agency in the U.S. knew them. I thought they would surely know of opportunities that would fit me and could make an intro.

My gut was right. The business growth guru was instrumental in making connections for me in various parts of the country with multiple opportunities. Unfortunately, one potentially lucrative and prestigious opportunity quickly turned sour as one of their key clients was a large tobacco manufacturer. Marketing tobacco violated my "How would I explain this to my four-year-old?" rule without trying to be a prude. I felt like if I couldn't openly talk to my little boys about what their daddy was marketing, I couldn't market it. When I told the head of the agency this, he tried to persuade me that I could sell it in good conscience since they focused their marketing efforts on third-world countries. He may have been able to justify that to *his* kids, but I couldn't. I was in a pickle. I was desperate to separate from my partner as soon as possible as it was becoming increasingly risky for me to stay, knowing the damning information I'd uncovered about him.

Thrive/Wither Clue: I "thrive" when I'm selling something I believe in and when I can openly talk about whatever I'm selling with my young children. That is more important to me than resolving an immediate financial need.

Ironically, this gut-wrenching time where I had to face walking away from my own company that gave me validation, balance, recognition, and a sense of community spawned something. It drove me to create my first draft of what I call the "Thrive/ Wither Exercise." This bonehead-simple T-chart has surprisingly unlocked *many* friends, colleagues, management teams, and CEOs. As I opened this book with my friend's advice, "Out of our greatest painful struggles often emerges our greatest blessing to others," I hope that the pain that gave birth to my Thrive/Wither exercise will be a blessing to you. (If you didn't already carve out 30 minutes to do the Thrive/Wither exercise—Weapon #2—as outlined in Chapter 2, please do!)

CHAPTER 11

YOU CAN RUN,
BUT YOU CAN'T HIDE

"This idea that you're undeserving, a fraud—that you're
not as smart or as talented or 'together' as people might
think makes you an 'imposter' and therefore unqualified
in whatever it is you want to do and someday you're going
to be found out. By whom? The imposter police?"

– Anthony Meindl

I knew I had to leave Wichita but exactly where was in question. It was clear that being near my mentor in New York or Minneapolis (he split time between cities as he had homes and offices in both) wasn't going to work for my family. New York was far too big. Minneapolis was far too cold—my wife had a physical condition at the time that extreme cold exacerbated. I went back to my notes in my Thrive/Wither exercise. I'd written down, "Pleasant Location—Weather, scenery, proximity to relatives, recreation activities." That would prove to be critical in evaluating an opportunity that the business growth guru brought to me out of the blue while I was in Kansas City inter-viewing with a large ad agency.

Cell phones weren't as prevalent as they are now, and I didn't have one. Nevertheless, I ensured that the business growth guru always knew how to reach me since I was increasingly desperate to find my ticket out of the agency that included my name on the door. Surprisingly, he called me while I was in KC at my in-laws and said he wanted me to book a direct flight the next day from KC to Charlotte, NC. He had a small agency willing to give me equity if I proved to be the right fit. I'd never been to North Carolina, much less Charlotte, but I trusted him. I wasn't interested in a smaller agency than my own, but I fell in love with the beauty of Charlotte and could see my fam-ily flourishing there.

Thrive/Wither Clue: A pleasant location is vital to me when considering a career move—weather, scenery, proximity to relatives, and recreation activities matter.

After my first meeting with this prospective Charlotte-based firm, I flew the owner and his wife to Wichita to see the agency I'd rebuilt. The several months of professional courtship also included me flying to Charlotte to help his team pitch busi-ness. I thought I'd done an excellent job in assessing "fit." I even interviewed each member of the firm, asking if there was anything I needed to know before I moved my wife and two young boys (ages 7 and 4) halfway across the country. We were seven hours away from our closest family members, so I felt I needed to be extra cautious about making a sound decision. All the signs looked like we were making the right move. Tragically, I couldn't have been more mistaken.

I'd delivered a multi-million-dollar aerospace account to my new "partner," and my top designer also followed me to this little design firm. The first week in my new office, our head of account service and the office manager came to me independently to warn me of the same thing. "You have no idea what you just got into. The owner is abusive, and that is why his wife is leaving the company to save their marriage. I'm so sorry you moved your family across the country for this."

Stunned, I responded, "Why didn't you say something to me when I asked if there was anything I needed to know before I made such a major move when I interviewed you individually?"

"The owner told us that if anyone screwed up this deal, we'd be found out and fired on the spot," was the reply from each of them.

I was shocked by their revelations. A couple of lessons learned from this encounter:

1. You can *never* do too much due diligence prior to making a major move.
2. Even good people will withhold important information when a gun is held to their head.

I thought, "Surely, I can make this work. I *have* to make it work." But, as I knew it would only add more stress to a stressful move, I couldn't tell my wife about this devastating news.

It would simply be too much for her as we were still acclimating to a new city.

Six months later, after the client had approved all our design work and we'd executed a year's worth of media buys for this big client, my "partner" called me into his office. He told me that it was my last day. He waited for my designer to be away on his honeymoon to pull the trigger and unceremoniously fire me. My partner also owed me tens of thousands of dollars in commissions. While he remained in the room, he told me to immediately call my big client and tell them I was resigning. He assumed I'd go away quietly. He knew I'd forgiven hundreds of thousands of dollars from my previous partner, so he didn't think I'd make a fuss over tens of thousands.

Thrive/Wither Clue: I "thrive" when I'm in a place where integrity matters and I have someone I can learn from in the organization.

Without warning, I was back in search mode *again*. I didn't know many people in Charlotte at the time. Our savings account was pathetically minuscule. My wife was a stay-at-home mom raising our two little boys. I was depressed. I was desperate.

I met with practically every other design firm and ad agency owner in the city, hoping to land something. *No one was interested*—primarily because I'd been president of my firm, and my previous salary had been higher than what most creative directors in town were making. So, I frantically started looking at other markets. As hard as I tried, I kept coming up with nothing. Zero. Nada. Zilch. That's when fate struck again with the "soccer dad" experience on the sidelines of the YMCA soccer fields that I recalled in the Introduction section of this book.

I was shocked that the Fortune 500 bank that my new "soccer dad" friend introduced me to hired me despite my resume. Yes, the bank wanted someone with my advertising background, but had it not been for my new soccer dad friend, there's no way my resume would have made it in front of the SVP who hired me. My father, a man who'd been an educator all his life, was thrilled that I was finally out of the volatile ad agency world. I called him after my first day at orientation. I don't know if the other 100 people or so who were in that orientation session with me were as shocked as I was or not, but the HR person delivered a transparently honest message that even blew away my father when I conveyed it to him.

The HR person said, "It used to be that if you were competent in your job, you could retire from banking after decades of service with a gold pocket watch and a pension. Those days are gone. We identified a specific set of skills we need that each of you possesses. There are no guarantees we'll need those skills tomorrow. So do yourself a favor: take advantage of our training programs and add to your skillset 'toolbox' as long as you are here."

That was a profound move for a company to be that honest in 1995—long before the gig economy was a thing.

I took the HR person's advice and took all the training programs I could. I was grateful for the ability to pay my bills and have a job. I also liked a lot of the people who were my colleagues. But soon, I started coming home grumpy every night.

It was my first time in a large, publicly traded corporation, and it felt like a foreign land. It seemed like the bank's COO relished seeing his EVPs go to war with each other to take more turf. It was like witnessing pit bull fights on a routine basis. I thought it created an unnecessarily caustic corporate culture. The problem: those of us stuck in middle management needed to get stuff done. I hated the highly charged CYA (Cover Your A**) political environment, the difficulty of getting anything done, and the fact that I was just another cog in the machine. I was *so* far away from where I'd seen my most satisfying success: the design and advertising world.

Thrive/Wither Clue: I "wither" whenever I'm just another body or cog in the wheel and stuck in a cubicle.

Fortunately, my wife lovingly but firmly told me I needed to find *something* to be grateful for in this new job. She was tired of my sour attitude. It was wearing out the entire family. She was right. Even though I felt I was so far from where I *should* be (running a design firm or ad agency), I needed to find meaning and purpose in what seemed to be a dead end for my career.

I quickly turned my focus from the stuff I didn't like to find meaning and opportunities in my situation. I remembered my love for forging long-term relationships, building bridges (even between warring factions), and solving problems. There were plenty of good people there, lots of opportunities to build bridges, and a plethora of issues needing to be solved. Unfortunately, I wasn't any closer to getting back into the design or advertising agency world. Still, I found meaning and purpose again in an environment I had previously deemed caustic. My mood shifted.

Thrive/Wither Clue: I "thrive" when I'm forging solid and long-term relationships (people-oriented) and whenever I'm making things work better, fixing problems, creating new opportunities, and building businesses and brands.

I couldn't do anything about the EVP dog fights occurring well above my colleagues and me, but I could move the ball forward with colleagues in different silos that also needed to get stuff done. I was amazed at how myopic our 40,000-employee company could be. It seemed like the right hand didn't know what the left hand was frequently doing. We had various bank departments hitting the same customers with conflicting offers and messages. We were stumbling over our own feet. We weren't creating a good customer experience. (Quite the contrary!) Building bridges across these warring factions was easy to do when we focused on the customer versus the turf our respective EVPs were fighting to defend or seize.

When I focused on the stuff that made me come alive (things in my thrive zone), I transcended my longing to be back in an industry where I'd seen success (the advertising and design world) and the caustic culture of the bank. I started having fun again. Then, out of the blue, I got a call from a much larger, competing Fortune 100 bank down the street. One of my current colleagues who that bank was recruiting mentioned my name when they discussed the need to fill a non-traditional "MacGyver" role. She thought they were describing me to a "T." Had I not given my word in agreeing to take the meeting, I wouldn't have shown up for the interview. I'd accepted a cease-fire in my mind for pushing to get back in the ad agency world, but going to another bank that had a reputation for aggressive market expansion? No, thank you.

CHAPTER 12

THE IMPOSTER IS EXPOSED—AGAIN

"Even though I had sold 70 million albums, there I was feeling like 'I'm no good at this.'"

– Jennifer Lopez

Only out of respect for my colleague who recommended me to the Fortune 100 bank and the fact that I'd committed to the interview, I went. I thought that I'd politely show up, leave, and that would be that. I wasn't interested in another detour in banking, so far from my industry of choice—advertising.

During the interview, I was surprised by how much I initially liked the people I met and how the role they described seemed like my next step. It sounded like it would certainly be challenging and fun. Surprisingly, things critical to the position were smack-dab in the middle of my thrive zone.

This Fortune 100 bank had just completed the largest bank acquisition in history at the time. While they were experts at M&A deals up and down the East Coast, this eleven-state acquisition in the Midwest proved problematic. Client attrition levels were higher than their accepted norms, and other metrics were way off. They were seeking someone from the Midwest with an extensive ad agency background. They needed someone good at building bridges between groups of people and, as one of the interviewers mentioned, a problem-solving "MacGyver."

After multiple rounds of interviews with numerous stake-holders, they offered me the job. I was thrilled for a very brief moment until I had to complete a thorough background check. (I wasn't worried about the background check, though.) However, explaining my employment gaps and revealing that I was a college dropout made my palms sweat. I'd managed to avoid those employment gaps and educational deficiencies up until this point. My childhood nightmares of showing up to class naked when everyone else had clothes on had become my reality. It was no longer a bad dream. The irony is this Fortune 100 bank said they wanted me for the things I was good at delivering, but I figured that surely, they wouldn't want me after they discovered I'd been massively duped twice, been unemployed, and the fact I was a college dropout.

After completing the form with my work and educational history in front of my new boss, I wanted to run away and cry. My first day hadn't even begun, and I already felt lower than a snake's belly. I asked her, "Why did you hire me? The job requirements are a college degree (master's degree preferred). I'm a college dropout. I've been unemployed. I've also been so blind that I got conned by trusted 'partners' more than once."

I was exposed and ashamed. My imposter syndrome was buck naked in the room. I wanted to slither out the door and hide.

She paused, smiled, and told me, "I'm not good at many things, but I checked you out thoroughly. I like building diversity in my teams. I like your non-traditional background. I look for people who've been kicked in the teeth more than once and keep getting up. I like humble, hungry street fighters. You're going to do great here."

Thrive/Wither Clue: I "thrive" being in charge of something and feeling valued for my ability to contribute versus my pedigree.

Before my first day began, the Fortune 100 bank did a reorganization. (I soon discovered this would be a routine occurrence as we'd experience two more massive acquisitions—the three largest bank acquisitions in history at the time would occur in under three years.) My hiring boss wasn't going to be my boss. Another powerful female exec would be. What I learned about myself, leadership, cultures, and life from these two women during the next few years could be enough to fill another book or two.

On my first day on the job, meeting with my new boss for the first time was probably the most profound meeting I've ever had. I wrote about it also on LinkedIn, and over 7.9 million people read that before the algorithm tapered off. The following summarizes that deeply impactful meeting...

My boss welcomed me into her office and shut the door. I had no idea that the meeting was about to deliver the impact of a hand grenade.

"Welcome to *our* company. We're glad you're here," she greeted me.

She quickly moved to a topic sacred to her and to the company: Core Values. She smiled but took on a serious tone. She said, "We stand for three things: 1) Do the Right Thing; 2) Teamwork and Trust; 3) Have a Passion for Winning—in that order."

It wasn't marketing gibberish. These were expected and rewarded behaviors here. She continued, "My job is to ensure the CEO knows who Gary Frey is. Once you've built your team, your job is to make sure that I know who your stars are. Hire your replacement and never be afraid to hire people smarter than yourself."

Servant Leadership: She didn't just talk about it. She *lived* it. She led by example.

Her peers and the CEO recognized her for it. She had the most coveted object in our company tucked away on her shelf: a Waterford° crystal hand grenade. She never mentioned it. She didn't have to. It was legendary. A precious few were given by the CEO to associates who had "jumped on the grenade" on behalf of our associates and customers.

She remains the best boss I've had. My takeaway: Know your core, lead by example, and when necessary, "jump on the grenade."

It is clear why this 1300-character post that I wrote 20 years after the event went viral. Leaders like that inspire people around the world. Leaders like that call their people to greatness. They don't just "talk the talk." They "walk the walk." They are rare. It was no wonder why I flourished working for her.

As much as I thought I'd dealt with my imposter syndrome, it wasn't silenced. It seemed as though once I quickly rose to the rank of Senior Vice President (SVP), my inner imposter syndrome would awaken and say, "Most of your peers have advanced degrees. You don't even have your bachelor's degree!"

My incredible boss could read me like a book. She repeatedly told me, "We have more confidence in you than you do." I wanted to run through brick walls for her every time she said that. It didn't necessarily set me free totally from imposter syndrome, but it quieted it a bit.

During our regular one-on-one meetings after I'd been at the bank for a couple of years, I told her that I'd love to participate in Harvard's Executive MBA program. I knew of another colleague the bank sponsored to participate in that program. She was all for it. I thought, "Perhaps, this program (and credential) could help me leapfrog over my educational deficiency and put a dagger in the heart of my imposter syndrome." Unfortunately, it wasn't meant to be. Internal budget cuts were issued before she could complete the paperwork, and my lifeline to my coveted educational shortcut was severed.

Even though I had but a few years working for this extraordinary leader, her many examples of how a healthy leader coaches, mentors, encourages, motivates, and leads probably impacted me more than any other leader I've served.

Thrive/Wither Clue: I "wither" when I don't have someone from whom I can learn within the organization. In this instance, I "thrived" primarily because of this outstanding leader and all she taught me.

CHAPTER 13

WHEN IT'S TIME TO LEAVE AN INSPIRING LEADER

> "To truly return, we must belong (and that man came to understand that he no longer belonged to the place he'd left as a sixteen-year-old boy)."
>
> – Jorge Galán

As mentioned in the previous chapter, I learned more about leadership while working for this powerful female leader than any other leader I've served. I thrived there because of it and quickly rose through the ranks—primarily because of her mentorship.

As is the way of many Fortune 100 companies, we seemed to reorganize before anyone could get very comfortable in their role. Perhaps that is one of the reasons I liked my brief few years at this company; something was constantly changing. In less than two years, we had completed the three largest acquisitions in U.S. banking history at that time. We went from 80,000+ "associates" (employees) when I started there to 160,000+ associates by the time I took an expanded role that included managing bicoastal teams—one in Charlotte, NC, and one in San Francisco, CA.

As I embraced those expanded opportunities, I often spent 1-2 weeks/month (never back-to-back weeks) away from home to be with my San Francisco team. I loved the dynamics of our group, the challenge of building something significant, the variety of office locations in San Francisco, and being able to enjoy the unique beauty of that part of the country. I didn't feel like I was simply thriving; I was soaring.

Thrive/Wither Clue: I "thrive" where there's variety—in tasks, travel opportunities, people interactions/clientele.

The success that my team and I enjoyed caught the attention of the company's highest ranks (likely because my boss promoted it). As part of our routine "catch-up" meetings, she presented me with an "opportunity" that was another step up the corporate ladder for me and my career at the company. They wanted me to expand my role to "positively infect the culture" of our recent acquisition and move my family to San Francisco.

As much of an honor and career booster as this new promotion would be, I had some real concerns:

1. The cost-of-living difference between Charlotte, NC and San Francisco was enormous in 1999. (It's even

more now.) So, the bump in salary and benefits weren't even close to making such a move make any financial sense as much as the Human Resources (HR) department ultimately tried to convince me otherwise.

2. The distance from my family was too great for me. Routinely traveling to California was one thing. Moving them across the country even further from family than the last time I was in this position when I declined the move to Scottsdale over a decade earlier.

3. Uprooting my pre-teen and teenage sons from their friends and schools into a vastly different city weighed heavily upon me.

I asked her if moving to San Francisco was a requirement for the promotion. She said it was. I asked her, "If I chose not to take the position, could I take on another role in the company?"

She said there were no guarantees and likely no open roles that would be right for me. However, she knew this role was perfect for me and would elevate my visibility even more with the top brass. I asked for some time to discuss it with my wife and sons as it was a big decision. She told me I had a little time, but I needed to decide before the end of the year—just a few months away.

My wife and I labored over this decision. I couldn't get any peace about it. I was in conflict. I knew it was a great move for my career and didn't want to disappoint my all-time favorite boss. It would be another opportunity to prove that a college dropout from the middle of Kansas could run with the big dogs. (Imposter syndrome was knocking again in my head.) But, at the same time, as much as I tried to convince myself that my sons would adjust just fine, my spirit was tormented. I knew I would have to decline the career advancement and, in essence, cut my throat at that company.

So, I decided I might need to pay more attention to those calls from various headhunters. It wasn't that I had them every day, but I was still in my 30s, working for a respected and innovative Fortune 100 that was making lots of waves, and I managed tens of millions in marketing dollars. So, I started taking those headhunter calls and meetings. I felt disloyal for doing so, but I believed I had to as time was running out before I had to disappoint my boss by declining the move.

I thought that if I were going to keep my imposter syndrome in check, I'd need to return to the ad agency or design firm world. I'd somehow captured the attention of a risk-taking hiring manager at this Fortune 100 company and overcome the educational requirements, but that wasn't likely going to be a repeat performance. Confirmation of my assumptions came quickly.

A large pharmaceutical company called. While I wasn't jumping up and down to go work for big pharma, the money was very tempting. I'd stay on the East Coast and begin working for a respected brand that spent a ton of money on advertising. Unfortunately, that little bit of mental gymnastics was short-lived. I didn't make it past the second interview when the recruiter needed clarification on my educational status. I had only listed my university, scholarship, GPA, and achievements on my resume. But I didn't include a degree earned. I explained why I dropped out after my sophomore year, ending the discussion quickly. My lack of a four-year college degree was a no "ifs, ands or buts" non-starter with this company. Interview over.

Shortly after that brief discussion with the big pharma recruiter, I had a speaking engagement in New York. (It wasn't because I was a great speaker, but because I worked for a notable brand with a large marketing budget.) Also, a prestigious headhunter knew I would be in the city for a few days. The headhunter wanted to meet over lunch, as he had a role that he wanted to discuss with me. I wondered if that might be the lifeline I was going to need. I committed to taking the meeting and was excited to do so.

On my last morning in New York, one of my friends, who was one of the event sponsors I spoke at, asked if I could join him for lunch—the same time I had committed to meeting with the prestigious headhunting firm. I was in conflict again. On the one hand, the prestigious headhunting firm likely had my safety net—a promising new job ready for me. On the other hand, my friend's wife had just received a dire and scary medical diagnosis, and I could tell it was weighing heavily on him. As much as I felt the pressure to find a job before turning down the relocation opportunity to San Francisco, I thought joining my friend for lunch during his challenging season was more important.

I called the headhunter and apologized for canceling the lunch-time interview with them, but I needed to be with a friend more. They were gracious even though I was canceling without much notice and declining a potential opportunity.

Thrive/Wither Clue: I "thrive" in forging strong, long-term relationships. Relationships trump accomplishments. Relationships trump opportunities.

Little did I know that choosing to honor something so crucial in my thrive zone (a valuable relationship) was about to be one of the most remarkable, career-impacting lunch meetings of my life to date.

CHAPTER 14

THE BLESSING WHEN OTHERS SEE PAST THE IMPOSTER

> "I wonder if anyone really identifies as the
> adult they've morphed into."
>
> – Emily Austin

Even though it has been over two decades since that lunch appointment occurred, I can still remember the magic of that beautiful fall meeting in Central Park's Tavern on the Green with my friend. I thought I was choosing to support my friend over a potential job opportunity. However, instead, an experience that would surprise both of us was awaiting.

As we enjoyed the breathtaking outdoor dining setting in Central Park, our conversation progressed from an encouraging recent update on his wife's condition to discussions about our families and business. He was the publisher of the largest business journal within a 41-market portfolio of business journals headquartered in Charlotte. Since I spent a lot of advertising money across those 41 publications, I asked if he could get me some concrete cost-of-living data on San Francisco. I didn't believe the cost-of-living data the bank's HR department used for my proposed relocation package. He said that was no problem, but wondered why I needed that info. I told him the bank wanted me to take a promotion requiring me to relocate to San Francisco. At that point, the conversation became surreal to both of us.

He shifted his gaze from my eyes to my forehead and moved his eyes back and forth as if he was reading something. Then, finally, he broke the brief silence of awkwardness and exclaimed, "You're the guy!"

I asked, "I'm the guy? What in the world are you talking about?"

Excitedly, he responded, "It's like a neon sign is going across your forehead. You're the guy!"

I thought the pressure he was facing had gotten to him, and he was in the midst of a breakdown right before me. I started to worry.

He continued, "We've got a national search for a president of this new online publishing entity, and *you* are the guy to run it!"

Now I knew he was crazy. He had been a former advertising agency guy as well, with a critical leadership role in one of the largest agencies in the world when he lived in L.A. Our shared experience in the agency world was one of the reasons that we could relate to each other so well. He moved from running an office of a large, prestigious ad agency to running a successful publication in one of the country's largest markets, but I couldn't see myself making that switch *at all.*

I said, "If you were telling me that I was the guy to go run an ad agency, I'd agree with you, but run an online publishing company? I have *zero* experience or credentials necessary for that." So then, I started explaining the many reasons in my mind why I had no business in even being considered for such a role.

He interrupted and outlined three reasons he was sure I was "the guy" to run this online entity. He identified three critical areas of expertise this online publishing company needed in this top spot:

1. **Branding.** The online entity's name made sense for the holding company, but did not correlate with any of the 41 publications. The new entity needed a rebranding effort. It needed a name and identity that these 41 publications would embrace as a cohesive extension of their brands rather than being identified with the holding company. I'd spent 16 years building brands up to this point; I had a track record.

2. **Bridge Building.** In 1999, any "dot-com" version of a "brick-and-mortar" company was often worth far more than the profitable "brick-and-mortar" company— even though the online entities routinely hemorrhaged *huge* money. Forty-one publishers felt threatened by the holding company's Chairman and CEO's decision to create and spin off a separate online entity. The president of the online entity would need to build bridges with 41 publishers who had lots of autonomy to run their individual publications as their own business

within the umbrella of the holding company. Finding win-win-win solutions for the respective journals, the online entity, and the holding company was critical for success. I was known for being a good bridge builder even across warring factions within large organizations.

3. **Business turnaround.** While this wasn't a business turn-around situation, the holding company needed someone who could take a three-person staff of the online entity and grow it into a substantial company. I had a track record with my first business turnaround in Kansas. I had a track record of building businesses and growing healthy teams in big companies. This company spent money judi-ciously, so having a scrappy (and thrifty) leader build the business wisely was essential to them.

Thrive/Wither Clue: Whenever someone else states things from your "thrive" zones without reading your Thrive/Wither document, *pay attention!* As a friend says, "It's hard to read the label when you're inside the jar."

Even though I still didn't think I was "the guy" my friend was seeking, he made a compelling argument that rang my bell as all three of his points were in my thrive zone. He could see that he'd disarmed me. Before I could mount another defense, he said I had three days to think about it before he followed up with me. Finally, he told me that if I were at least 40%

interested, he would make the intro to the Chairman and CEO of the parent company.

As soon as I boarded the flight back to Charlotte, my mind was racing with ideas. I couldn't shut off the flow of ideas as much as I firmly believed I was *not* "the guy." I compiled and typed all my thoughts onto two pages before my friend called me three days later as he had promised. When he called, I told him about my thought-flooding experience. Even though we were simply talking on the phone, I could see him smiling through the call.

It took some time to get onto the Chairman's schedule, but when the day arrived, I went to the YMCA to change into a suit knowing the Chairman was a rather formal guy, and our dress code at the big bank was dress casual. As soon as I signed in at the security desk, someone escorted me to the Chairman's boardroom. (Security was far tighter at this publication than what we had at one of the largest banks in the U.S. at that time!)

Once we got past the pleasantries, the Chairman was all business. The only reason I was there? My friend's strong recommendation. Indeed, my credentials didn't warrant it. I'm confident my resume wouldn't have seen the light of day if I had submitted it online.

Nonetheless, he reviewed my resume and asked some thoughtful questions, specifically about the three primary strengths my friend used to convince me to apply. Once we got through those questions, I told the Chairman I had a two-page document of thoughts I'd compiled given their current situation. He asked to see it. As I passed it across the massive conference table, I started to doubt why I was there and what I was doing, giving him a document filled with potentially stupid ideas. I began to sweat. (This seems to be a pattern in stressful situations when I'm trying to keep the imposter at bay.)

The Chairman was a hardcore newspaper mogul. He had been the president of Dow Jones. As he read my document, my mind started tormenting me with thoughts such as: "What was I thinking? Why in the world was I in his boardroom? Why would I humiliate myself by giving such an accomplished journalist my thoughts in written form?" I was confident I was likely in the most embarrassing career interviews up to that point in my life.

As I was fixated on his facial expressions, wondering if I should bolt for the door, I saw a glimpse of a smile start to appear with an ever-so-slight head nod. As he continued to the second page, more slight smiles and head nods ensued. I don't remember much of what else he said as I was in the middle of mental whiplash. I *do* remember that he offered me a job and nearly doubled my salary from the Fortune 100—right there on the spot! While the massive bump in pay was exciting, that paled in comparison to the fact that I could keep my family in Charlotte and not uproot my sons from their friends.

As excited as I was to stay in Charlotte and begin a new adventure in running a "dot-com" at the peak of the "dot-com" craziness, I dreaded telling my favorite boss, who had taught

The Blessing When Others See Past the Imposter   101

me so much, that I was leaving the bank. While she was disappointed that I was leaving a significant advancement at the bank, she was supportive. She threw me the best going away party (and fun-filled roast) I've experienced. I figure she had a score to settle with me as I'd recently pulled off the best April Fool's pranks I've ever done at her expense. She was tough, fair, and good-natured. She allowed me to bring my quirky sense of humor to a relatively stiff corporate environment.

True to her fantastic leadership form, she threw a going-away party for me in the form of a roast. She and my colleagues dressed me in an orange prison jumpsuit and had a blast roasting me at our favorite Mexican restaurant one night after work. She made sure she had the last good-natured laugh to pay me back for my April Fool's fake resignation that almost gave her a heart attack, among other fun-loving pranks I helped instigate during my brief tenure there. We worked hard. We played hard. We genuinely loved working as a team.

Thrive/Wither Clue: I "thrive" in environments that provide the freedom to be myself—with my quirky sense of humor and all.

CHAPTER 15

BUBBLES OFTEN BURST

**"What if you're wrong and you're not
an imposter?"**

– Dr. Jessamy Hibberd

Transitioning from a Fortune 100 company to building a team from the three original people who the Chairman of this business journal empire had tasked to start this online entity was exhilarating. The dot-com world was on fire, and I frequently worked late into the night, emailing my second-in-command, whom the Chairman had hired to provide the industry knowledge and deal-making expertise I didn't have. I had been alerted to my second-in-command's sensitivity that I was named president while he received the EVP title. As a result, I always referred to him as my partner and treated him as such. He knew the industry and was very good at selling via revenue-generating partnerships. I figured that as long as I stayed in my lanes of rebranding the company, building bridges by finding win-win solutions with the 41 publishers threatened by this separate entity, and growing the team into a stand-alone company, all would be good.

My Chairman was an accomplished businessman, an industry-leading visionary, and a journalist of few words. He was tough but fair. He liked the dynamic duo he'd put in place between myself and my partner, the EVP. He knew how to identify talent and give us a healthy mix of freedom and responsibility while holding us accountable. I had to adjust from managing tens of millions of dollars at the big bank to arm wrestling my Chairman for even ten thousand dollars for marketing in this fledgling entity. I was used to being a creative street fighter from my first turnaround, so it wasn't a huge deal. However, being resource-constrained can often unleash the most incredible level of creativity. I wasn't running a creative firm, but I didn't need to do that to have fun. Having a role that allowed me to creatively rebrand our company with minimal resources while finding win-win solutions that worked for our subscribers, publishers, and the rapidly growing team was exhilarating. We were agile, frugal, and given the freedom to build something incredible.

Thrive/Wither Clue: I "thrive" in situations that are more idea-generating and less paper-generating.

Our company was established as a separate entity from the 41 business publications and the holding company to give us flexibility in a hot Initial Public Offering (IPO) market. However,

I didn't join this company for the promise of becoming filthy rich in case the Chairman decided to take this entity public. Instead, I took the job because it allowed me and my family to stay in Charlotte while tapping many things in my thrive zone. I'm grateful that I had that perspective as I quickly became surrounded by CEOs and key execs who experienced *huge* pay-days in that surreal dot-com world.

I could write another book or two just about the crazy things I saw and experienced during the "dot-com" boom and bust. However, one of the most profound experiences was when my Chairman asked me to develop a relationship with the Founder and the CEO of a competitive entity in San Francisco. Our holding company had invested $1 million in that company. My Chairman believed in keeping competitors close and investing in a leading one in our competitive space made sense to him. I had numerous trips to San Francisco to meet with these two leaders, and it seemed like each time, my mind got blown even more than the previous trip.

On one of my first trips to meet with them at their offices, I was overwhelmed with the amount of costly, massive flat-screen TVs, the number of people they had working for them, and the sheer amount of overhead they were carrying in some pricey digs in San Francisco. I was astonished when I found out that this company was burning through approximately $40 million per year on $1 million in top line sales. To make it even more mind-blowing, I asked the Oxford-educated CEO what their business model was. With a grin, he said, "Well, Gary, it's a very nimble business model driven by eyeballs." (That's *exactly* what he said, word-for-word. I'll never forget it.)

My matter-of-fact, "I'm just a simple dude from Kansas," response was, "So, what you are saying is that you don't have a formal business model per se, but your business model is driven by advertising revenue."

He quickly responded with his British accent behind another grin, "Precisely."

Almost as soon as I returned home to Charlotte from this meeting, I was beckoned back to San Francisco to meet with them again. They wanted me to meet some investment bankers as well. They had a potential deal they wanted to discuss with me. Once I was with them again, they broke the news to me. They had just sold out to a major media company for $225 million. As the CEO gleefully exclaimed, "We're *rich!*" They wanted to buy a minor stake in our conservatively managed and growing company for tens of millions of dollars. They asked me to be their guest at a celebratory party that included San Francisco's "Who's Who" at one of the Founder's new restaurants. It was like attending a "Lifestyles of the Rich and Famous" TV show for this small-town Kansas boy. The whole experience was surreal to witness.

I returned to Charlotte and met with my Chairman to convey the news of their massive liquidity event. I also relayed their offer to take a minority equity stake in our company. He seemed to be as mystified as I was. I started doubting everything we were doing by running our company like a real company by spending less money than we made. Finally, I told him, "I feel like the world is upside down. In this new dot-com world, it seems like the more money you lose, the more valuable the company is to Wall Street." He wanted time to think over this news and their unexpected offer to buy a stake in our company.

A couple of weeks later, he called for a meeting with me and told me he didn't want to take their offer. He had a feeling that the dot-com bubble was inevitable and didn't believe that the company making an equity offer to us would be around in two years.

Sure enough, the dot-com bubble burst. The CEO, Founder, and some key employees at that competitive company did well, but the company (along with many dot-coms at that time) eventually imploded. Many hopeful employees suddenly were unemployed, and stock options they thought would be worth millions quickly became worthless. My Chairman called the dot-com bubble collapse to the month. Wise man. No wonder he'd experienced such success. He was no fool. We weren't rich, but our company didn't collapse. (As of this writing, it's still thriving 23 years after the dot-com bubble burst!)

As we continued to grow judiciously, my deal-making partner (the EVP) eventually struck gold with one of the world's largest tech companies. They were interested in taking a minority equity stake in our company for tens of millions of dollars, like the company that had recently had the $225 million exit. As the terms of the deal got worked out over many months, it became apparent that even though this tech company had a minor stake in our company, they would be calling many of the shots. Consequently, many of the things that made me come alive in my thrive column were likely going to go away. My Chairman sensed this and proposed a role within the holding company that he thought would be enough to keep me engaged. While I loved working for him and the salary (and perks) were very generous, I knew inside that I'd likely be spending more time in my wither column than in my thrive zone.

Thrive/Wither Clue: I "wither" when I don't see the ability to make an impact or to make a difference typically present in slow, bureaucratic organizations.

Another fork in the road was right in front of me. I felt as if I stayed in that organization with a dramatic role change, I'd grow old prematurely. The problem was I didn't have another apparent option.

CHAPTER 16

SOMETIMES OPPORTUNITY KNOCKS (TWICE)

"I'm not a writer. I've been fooling myself and other people."

– John Steinbeck

Even though I had job security with the dot-com subsidiary of the large publishing company, I knew that things would change rapidly for me once the tech company deal got consummated. Most of the things I loved about my role as president of that company were going to be transferred back to the tech company in Seattle.

Shortly after we finalized that game-changing transaction, another seemingly innocent lunch conversation with a friend would change my trajectory again. Before I get into the gist of this particular conversation, we need to backtrack a few years. This lunch conversation was with a friend who was the CEO of a design firm that had been a creative vendor at the first big bank where I worked. When I was at the Fortune 100 bank, he asked me to serve as a growth consultant for his firm as a favor. I worked 60-70 hours per week at that Fortune 100 bank but working with this CEO and his leadership team one evening a month was fun for me.

We had fun together, and it must have made a difference because word got around. Another friend who had been named one of the top 50 creatives in the country asked if I could do some growth consulting for him as well. Very quickly, it was apparent that these two friends, who were running very different design and marketing firms, should meet as I saw that their firm's respective strengths complemented each other's weaknesses. Shortly after introducing them to each other, both CEOs saw the synergies and decided that merging their two firms was a great opportunity. They asked me to leave the Fortune 100 bank and join them as their third partner. I was flattered, but I quickly said, "No." I respected and loved both of them, but they knew the heartache I'd gone through from my first business partner's financial improprieties in Kansas, and I couldn't do that again.

Thrive/Wither Clue: I "thrive" in bringing an outside perspective to help build something unique—bringing an "outside the jar" ability to help those inside the jar "read the label."

That conversation was a couple of years before the lunch I referenced at the beginning of this chapter. As I disclosed my situation running the dot-com with the global tech partner was about to change things for me, my friend knocked on my door a second time. While I was busy growing the dot-com, my two friends who became business partners had been operating their combined companies as one company in two locations. They planned on getting the two teams under a common roof via a building both of my friends were purchasing. They offered me a third of the company to join as president.

After diving deeper into the respective roles and responsibilities that the three of us would have, I decided it was the right move for me. I announced my decision to my boss, the publishing company's Chairman, and he tried to talk me out of leaving. However, after he understood my reasons for leaving his much larger company to join a much smaller design firm, he graciously retained me to serve as his advisor for the next year as he knew I would take a pay cut when I left his firm. I'll forever be grateful for the opportunities he brought my way, even when I was no longer working for him as an employee.

As much as I enjoyed my job at the dot-com and the prior Fortune 100 bank, I found a new sense of freedom and joy I hadn't experienced since my first turnaround as president of this hot design firm. We had one of the country's most substantial collections of design talent. We had a nice variety of clientele who valued exceptional design and were willing to pay handsomely for it. We had a healthy culture with very hip offices as the building my partners bought had been a renovated industrial space that we converted to include an indoor basketball court with a cappuccino bar overlooking it. The company even had a twin-engine airplane. Most importantly, I was part of a team that I'd put up against anyone. Once again, I was sure this would be my "forever" career home.

Well, again, "forever" this side of heaven is temporary at best. Only about a year into my "forever" gig, tragedy struck one of my business partners. He had a very young son who was perplexing the doctors as he was physically regressing rapidly. The pressure of that, coupled with the financial pressures we were feeling after the tragedy of 9/11/2001, proved too much. Without going into the heartbreaking details, the two business partners I'd introduced to each other decided to split the company back into their two original companies. I was soon going to be president of a non-existent entity. Once again, the end of this road was fast-approaching.

CHAPTER 17

BIGGER ISN'T ALWAYS BETTER

"I wanted to make sure everything I said was perfect before I would chance saying anything, and often found myself hearing a guy saying what I had been thinking but was too afraid to say. I did learn fairly early on that my being quiet and not voicing opinions only served to create doubts in the minds of others about my abilities."

– Joyce Roché

Just when I felt like I'd returned "home" in a place where I fit at this wildly creative design firm, it was time to aggressively find a job again. Ugh. My NYC mentor's words were haunting me. He had told me in my early thirties, "This is a young man's business. Make sure you are where you want to be by age forty." My partners informed me that they had decided to split the company a month before my 40th birthday.

Bad news evidently travels fast and far. Shortly after I found out my partners were going to split our firm back into their original pieces, I received a call from a friend who was the CFO for the largest privately held ad agency in the U.S., based in Detroit, MI. He had heard about our firm splitting up and asked if the rumors were true. I confirmed that was the case. He wanted to know what I was going to do. I told him I wasn't sure as this news was relatively recent. He said, "Why don't you consider running our Cleveland, OH office?"

I'd been in their impressive Detroit office before, but I didn't even know they had a Cleveland office, much less anything about it. The story was that the guy running the Cleveland office was also running their Baltimore office and leading business development efforts for their headquarters in Detroit. But unfortunately, that guy was spread too thin.

I think the biggest reason I passed the smell test with the guy running the Cleveland office was that the CFO from headquarters wanted me in the seat. They eventually offered me the job requiring me to move our family from Charlotte to Cleveland, OH, the "Great White North." We settled into a small suburb on the east side of the city, smack-dab in the middle of the snow belt due to the formidable lake effect snows coming off Lake Erie. We chose the village of Chagrin Falls primarily because of the Blue-Ribbon Schools for our sons, who were in high school and middle school at the time.

I poured my heart and soul into that 100-person Cleveland office. I quickly realized that we had issues. Departments existed in silos. There was a palpable caste system in this office. We had big clients who weren't happy, and many employees weren't happy either. The signature gray skies of Cleveland seemed to permeate our culture as well. While the offices were very bright, sleek, and modern, the atmosphere in the company was territorial, non-collaborative and oppressive. It wasn't uncommon to witness someone publicly berate another employee with criticism over their creative work product or "sophomoric" thinking. The impressive hip and trendy office aesthetics couldn't conceal the dysfunctional and oppressive culture underneath.

Thrive/Wither Clue: I "wither" when I'm in a cutthroat, critical, and non-team-oriented culture.

Our office manager told me something that puzzled me one day. She said, "You bring 'light' here." She must have noticed the perplexed look on my face after she said it, so she continued, "I mean, you know everyone's names. You bring different groups together that haven't been part of the same meetings. You are fostering collaboration where it never existed before. That didn't happen under your predecessor."

While that made me feel good, change agents aren't always welcome by everyone. Only a year or so after I arrived, we shut down our Baltimore office, and the guy I came to replace quickly reclaimed the Cleveland office as his own. He was back in. Soon, I was out—again. Feeling like a stranger in a foreign, frozen land, I couldn't help but wonder, "What is wrong with me?"

CHAPTER 18

FINDING PURPOSE IN THE WILDERNESS

"I'm constantly doubting everything I've achieved, everything I'm working on business-wise and everything I'm working on in my personal life! (Even down to second guessing if I should have said certain things, or 'did I do that properly'...it's bloody annoying...)."

– Zoe Sugg

At the age of 42, I felt like I had taken so many wrong turns in my career that even with a GPS, I couldn't find my way back home. I was unemployed again and living in a city that constantly reminded me repeatedly, "You're not from here!" After the novelty of experiencing our first winter of over 100" of snow in Chagrin Falls, OH, the seemingly perpetual winter and depressing gray skies made me want to rename the Cleveland region, "Narnia." I told my wife and sons that I thought we should consider moving back to Charlotte, where sunshine, blue skies, and familiar friends were plentiful.

Thrive/Wither Clue: In my "thrive" column is "Pleasant Location—weather, scenery, proximity to relatives, and recreation activities." I apologize to my Cleveland friends; Cleveland didn't fit any of those requirements for me. The gray skies and distance from any relatives were tough on me.

To my surprise, my oldest son, who was in his junior year of high school, said he wasn't willing to move again. Moving from Charlotte to the Cleveland area was tougher on all of us than I thought it would be, so returning to Charlotte would be a welcome move—so I thought. However, since it wasn't, I needed to concentrate my efforts on finding something in Cleveland. Also, since Cleveland has long winters of brutal cold, networking with others during those winter months doesn't come as naturally as it does in Charlotte for some reason.

I don't remember how I connected with a local, successful marketing firm CEO. Still, I'll never forget the breakfast or the conversation with him, his business partner, and his growth coach. We were having breakfast at a popular, locally owned restaurant. The CEO somehow knew about my situation, and after hearing me tell more of my story, he said to the other two at the table, "Gary is relatively new to town. It's our responsibility to help him."

His statement followed up with action proved to be one of the warmest and brightest moments I've experienced in my career journey. Little did we realize that this breakfast meeting would lead to unexpected business relationships and enduring friendships.

The CEO initially hired me as his consultant, given some challenges his firm faced with a couple of their key accounts. Before I knew it, I was employed full-time and on the management team of the CEO's 140+ person company.

One of those two key accounts experiencing some challenges was a large, international tire manufacturer with its U.S. operations based in Los Angeles. I not only became close friends with our automotive-focused team, but I also earned the trust of the American management team of this Japanese tire manufacturer. The top American in the company introduced me to the Japanese CEO of the U.S. operations because they had a marketplace challenge that they thought I could help them address.

Without going into all the details, they needed my consulting skills and tapped in a big way to help this notable international tire manufacturer. The assignment utilized many of my passions and the expertise I had developed over the years. For example, they needed these skills: listening to employees, distributors, and customers; uncovering possibilities; creative problem-solving; getting teams aligned, focused, and executing against a common goal; and building long-term relationships based on results and trust. It was one of my all-time favorite assignments. (Plus, the frequent travel to L.A.'s warm, sunny climate during the cold and cloudy Cleveland winters was an added mood-enhancer.)

Thrive/Wither Clue: Based on this experience, I added this to my "thrive" column shortly after finishing this assignment: "Making things work better, fixing problems, creating new opportunities, building businesses and brands, elevating sales and customer experiences."

The outcome was so impactful that the top American of this international tire manufacturer told me they discussed hiring me away from my firm in Cleveland to run product development and marketing for them. I was deeply honored as both he and his CEO had become my friends. However, moving my family to L.A. wasn't going to work for my family or me. My oldest son was about to begin his freshman year in college in Kentucky, and there was no way I could consider forcing my family to move to the West Coast. A private equity firm I'd invested in a year prior had an unexpected offer that wouldn't require me to move. That out-of-the-blue purchase of my consultancy and job offer would eventually change my life.

CHAPTER 19

SOMETIMES OPPORTUNITY TAPS YOU ON THE SHOULDER, THEN GRABS YOUR WALLET

"I wonder if the secret of the social human is to tactfully conceal the fact that you're screaming on the inside."

– Robin Ince

When I began working in earnest with that international tire company in L.A., a local friend in Chagrin Falls introduced me to the Founder of a famous clothing line. This Founder sold his clothing company at a young age for a boatload of money and was now the Founder and CEO of a private equity company that was, in actuality, a by-invitation-only investment club at the time.

In this by-invitation-only investment club, an existing member had to "sponsor" or recommend a new member for that prospective member to get into the "club." Additional membership criteria required of the prospective member:

1. Accredited investor status.
2. Career had to include profit and loss (P&L) responsibility.
3. "High integrity, low ego" character.
4. A willingness to help others with no strings.

Without knowing it, I was being "recruited" into this exclusive club of approximately 300 high-net-worth families. Once I got invited to participate, I realized that while I technically met all the criteria, I was on the *bottom rung* of the ladder regarding the financial hurdles. I had no business being part of a group of such accomplished, wealthy, and in some cases, famous members of this group. Nonetheless, the Founder of this private equity group wanted me to join the group, which required a substantial financial investment. I was honored they invited me into the group. But while the size of investment needed to join the group was insignificant to most of our members given their vast wealth, it was *very significant* to me. Looking back, I had no business allocating the bulk of my savings to such an investment, but I did.

Within the first year of my investment, the Founder asked me to join his Advisory Board filled with some notable powerhouse people. He had recently hired a friend of mine (who would eventually be named CEO) to transform his company from a "by-invitation-only investment club" into a more robust private equity firm. They wanted to create a firm that behaved more like a full-service family office, with various services like sophisticated insurance offerings, more robust investment offerings, specialized financing services, etc. After one of our Advisory Board meetings, the Founder tapped me on the shoulder during dinner and said, "We have big plans for you." Shortly after, he told me they wanted to purchase my little consultancy with expertise in branding, business growth, and cultural compatibility assessments. In addition, he wanted me as a full-time member of his management team.

I was blown away by the opportunity, but the imposter syndrome within me was now on high alert. Imposter syndrome tormented my mind with questions like, "What if people found out I was a college drop-out? What if others in the group understood how little wealth I had? What if I became covetous of others once I realized how much wealth they had? How can I even relate to this class of people when I have no notable credentials?"

Even though those questions repeatedly tormented me, I somehow felt like destiny was calling. I loved working with business owners as I'd seen how far-reaching their impact could be—for good and not-so-good. I wanted to be with, learn from, and hopefully, in some way, help business owners. I also could grasp the kind of company the Founder and my friend wanted to build based on a unique chassis.

I agreed to their offer, and they gave me the most innovative title I've ever had: "Chief Impact Officer." It was unique and purposely ambiguous. The Founder and CEO wanted to give me lots of latitude across the organization to create a positive impact on our members, company, and employees.

In less than a year of selling my consultancy to the private equity firm, the Founder announced he would exit the company, and my friend from Chagrin Falls was named CEO. During this transition, the exiting Founder also asked me to take his role as "pledge master" (deciding what prospective members would be invited into and accepted into the group). By this time, I also realized that to do so, while being in full compliance with securities laws, I needed to get my securities licenses to have some of the financial discussions that the Founder was having.

As a result, I signed up to prepare for a series of arduous securities tests to get the proper licensing. The more I learned, the more I realized the severity and the sobriety of the responsibilities these licenses required. It was months of studying, practice tests, rote memorization, and review of formulas, rules, and regulations before I sat for my first six-hour test for one of the licenses. I was a basket case. I hated the subject matter. I was terrified by the immense responsibility that these securities licenses carried.

The only thing that kept me in the ring to endure what was required to pass those exams was my desire to be in regulatory compliance so I could have meaningful conversations with our members and prospective members. While we were a financial firm, the financial aspect of the job wasn't what mattered most to me; getting to know these members' stories intimately and finding ways to help them with the things that mattered most to them were the things that mattered most to me.

Thrive/Wither Clue: I "wither" in roles requiring lots of changing governmental rules, regulations, and compliance.

While I served as "pledge master" to determine who was allowed into the group as part of my role, I also had other responsibilities. I was responsible for selling securities, building out our "Life Services" division, evaluating potential acquisition targets, branding, communications, and hosting memorable events as part of our efforts to elevate and differentiate our member experience. Selling our private equity offerings was the *hands-down least favorite* part of my job. My favorite duties were expanding and developing our team, adding new products and services, forging strategic partnerships for our Life Services division, hosting memorable events, and connecting members to other resources to solve problems.

Being amongst such an accomplished group of ultra-wealthy people occasionally seemed to give a microphone to my inner imposter syndrome where I'd frequently hear it scream, "What are you doing in the same room with these people? The only thing that should be permitting you into the same room would be if you were a waiter!"

Ironically, this notion of being a "waiter" (serving someone else) led me to one of the most significant breakthroughs of my life in silencing that tormenting voice of the imposter. I covered this topic of focusing on serving others vs. how they perceive us in Chapter 4.

Thrive/Wither Clue: I "thrive" when I'm serving others. I've found that if my focus is on that simple act versus on how people perceive me, I'm in my happy place. However, as soon as I allow myself to compare myself with others versus serving them, I quickly drop into my "wither" zone. Again, comparison kills gratitude!

Just as I started to feel like I was hitting my stride inside this private equity firm, the earth began to shake under my feet. The first shock waves from the Great Recession hit on September 15, 2008, with a 504-point dive on the Dow Jones Industrial average. That day is permanently etched in my memory. The pilot commented about the dramatic stock market drop when I deplaned from a flight to one of our offices for a management team retreat. The pilot was shaken. Little did I know that tremor was minor compared to what we'd experience in the next 16 months in this company.

As our company began to falter, our Vice Chairman often closed out our increasingly depressing Leadership Team calls with, "Guys, I'm out. I've got to get my eyes off me and serve someone." Upon that statement, he'd leave the call and find a way to precisely do that. It wasn't an empty statement but a way of life for him. He'd seen the financial and corporate success many people dream of having, but that isn't what defined him in his mind or mine. He was a man of deep conviction, wisdom, and integrity. He exhibited a practical way of dealing with stress and destruction in a powerfully positive way.

I outlined in Chapter 5, the power of intentionally finding gratitude amid difficulties and the freeing discipline of writing in a gratitude journal. The summer of 2009 through the end of the year was the most intense and prolonged nightmare I've ever experienced. One of our Board members (who lost more when our company collapsed than any other member) proved to be a giant among leaders—even though he was the youngest one on the Board by decades. Frankly, his generosity kept me alive and ensured that the remaining "non-toxic" assets that had *any* value could be preserved before we could safely move them to another company. He sacrificed far more time and money than anyone else and was by my side amid the smoldering rubble.

This Board member became one of my very close friends. He asked me to meet him for breakfast over Thanksgiving week the following year. During that breakfast, he said something to me that revealed his depth of character and wisdom far exceeding his years. He said, "If someone told me, 'You get to choose. You can either have *all* your money back that you lost in that company without the lessons learned or the relationships forged. Or you can keep all the lessons learned and the relationships forged in that company without ever getting any of your money back,' it isn't even close. So, while losing all that money *really* hurts, I'd pick the lessons learned and relationships gained over those millions of dollars every day."

His words weren't simply empty platitudes. I saw him live out those words even when it cost him dearly. He never recovered one thin dime from the many millions he lost in that private equity firm. Yet, I saw him live out his faith and honor his words with intentional and sacrificial acts of integrity. His words inspired me. His actions raised the bar so high that his example challenges me to this day. I'll never be able to repay him for all he did for me, for how much he taught me, nor for what his friendship still means to me to this day.

Thrive/Wither Clue: While making money is important, it pales in comparison to forging quality, lasting relationships with people of integrity. I "thrive" when relationships come before making money.

CHAPTER 20

SOMETIMES, YOU FIND YOUR WAY BACK HOME

"I feel every time I'm making a movie, I feel like [it's] my first movie. Every time I have that same fear that I'm gonna be fired. And I'm not joking. Every movie, the first week, I always feel that they could fire me!"

– Penélope Cruz

As I've mentioned, the collapse of our private equity firm and the ensuing horrors was one of my life's most traumatic wilderness experiences. However, it was also one of the richest (not financially!) and most profound learning environments of my life. I wouldn't wish the horrors I experienced on my worst enemies, but like the Board member I mentioned, I wouldn't trade the transformational lessons I learned there *or* the friendships forged in the fires of adversity either.

From 2010 until 2015, the seemingly endless gray skies and winters that seemed to drag on without mercy in Ohio did their best to drain any lingering hope I had of returning home to the

Carolina-blue skies of Charlotte, NC. Then, in 2012, one of our private equity firm's Board members asked me to join one of his companies as it was struggling. By late 2014, I'd completed a sales turnaround of his insulating glass manufacturing company. That was another unexpected stop on my career journey where I felt *completely* unqualified to lead as I had *zero* prior experience in that industry before he asked me to join that company's management team. However, we grew the company back to profitability by God's grace, a lot of teamwork, and collaboration with customers who needed us to succeed as much as we needed to. Soon, that company no longer needed my services.

After I left the insulating glass manufacturing company, I did some sales and marketing consulting work for another manufacturing company in the area (a spray lubricant company) in early 2015. Shortly after I began that consulting assignment, we had another -20-degree F (ambient) day in February. When I arrived home one evening, my wife told me, "I can't take another winter up here. If I must live through another winter like this, I think I will die."

I knew exactly how she felt. Neither of us liked freezing weather, but we'd endured 13 winters in the Great White North of Cleveland, OH. We knew that somehow, we needed to make it back home to Charlotte. My wife had endured many terrifying twists and turns in my crazy career. She seemed to be saying to me, "Saddle up. Let's ride."

I finished my consulting contract with the spray lubricant company in April, and it was time to begin what I referred to as our "high-stakes treasure hunt." Searching for a job at the age of 53 isn't a short putt. Searching for a job at age 53 when you have a highly non-traditional career path, as I've had without a financial safety net, raises the difficulty level quite a bit. If you've ever held the title of "President" once (or four times like I have), it's often more of a curse than a blessing if you seek a job that's anything less than the top spot in an organization.

Nonetheless, my wife and I were determined to return to Charlotte, NC, one way or another. I figured that if we were going to be unemployed (we couldn't afford to do so for very long, though!), we might as well be unemployed in a city we knew and loved. Plus, Charlotte had much lower taxes and far better weather than we'd experienced in Ohio.

From my experience running companies in Charlotte, I knew those job applicants who merely *wanted* to move to the city had a far lower chance of being hired than local applicants. (Moving takes time, is disruptive, and is distracting—that's why most employers are far more interested in local applicants than those planning on relocating.) I couldn't afford *any* additional hurdles, so I told my wife, "I need to spend a couple of weeks in Charlotte to meet with people. I'll burn up the last of our Marriott points and stay with friends when the points run out." Fortunately, she was as committed as I was to return to Charlotte and cool with my plan.

As hard as I tried to schedule some meetings before embarking on the eight-hour drive down I-77 to Charlotte, I only had two meetings scheduled for my two-week job-seeking "treasure hunt." I spent the first night at a close friend's home north of the city and hit my knees the following morning as the reality of the situation hit me. "Please, Lord, don't let this trip be a bust. I only have two meetings scheduled. Both of those meetings are with business owner friends who don't have a job for me. Please open doors that only you can."

I had to use every one of the seven weapons discussed in this book to silence the imposter while on my mission to find a job back in Charlotte. I did my best to view this endeavor through the lens of an adventurous treasure hunt where I didn't know where the connections or clues might lead to a job that would fit me. However, I simply couldn't allow my mind to embrace the reality that I was 53, my crazy career path that wasn't easy to explain, or the fact that I was walking on a high wire without a financial safety net.

Even though I stayed in touch with many of my friends in Charlotte during my thirteen winters away in Ohio, none of them had a job for me. Plus, they still thought of me as a marketing guy who had run a successful publishing dot-com. Most didn't know much about my experience in private equity, manufacturing, or sales turnarounds while in Ohio. So, my "ask" of them was straightforward and without expectation. I started every conversation with something like this: "Jennifer and I are moving back home to Charlotte after 13 winters away—whether we have a job or not. I want to catch you up on what I've been doing and what I'm seeking. I'm not asking you for a job. If my story resonates and you think someone you know could be interested in my background, would you be willing to make an intro? I won't pressure them or embarrass you. I'm approaching this whole journey like a treasure hunt. I don't know where my next job is, but I'll eventually find it."

To my amazement, I had 30 in-person meetings during those two weeks—most of whom I didn't know simply because of the kindness of friends who made connections for me. Out of those meetings emerged a couple of job possibilities that seemed like they might turn into something. I drove home, told my wife about my experiences, and said, "Let's put the house on the market." She was all-in. We got a full asking price offer for the house within three days! After that, we needed to get ready for a move, and I had to head back to Charlotte for another couple of weeks. I needed to follow up with people who wanted to meet with me on my first trip, but our schedules didn't allow for us to meet.

I returned to Charlotte for another two-week "treasure hunting" trip. This time, I had 40 in-person meetings! One possibility dried up, but the other job possibility seemed to be gaining steam. A couple of my friends were so gracious to let me stay with them since I'd burned through my Marriott points. Even though the risks of not landing a job were always on my mind and the financial implications were frightening, I felt so alive. While I needed to find a job, I focused on seeing where I could help whoever met with me with connections they might need, encouragement, picking up the tab for the meal or coffee, etc. I truly wanted to focus on how I could serve them regardless of whether they could help me or not.

Our oldest son's wife gave birth to our second grandchild during that second two-week job-hunting trip. So, after I returned home to Ohio to wash clothes, help organize the house, and prepare for our upcoming move in July, we went to Kentucky to meet our newest grandson for a few days. Then, I packed up the car and jumped back on that windy stretch of I-77 back to Charlotte for my third two-week job-hunting trip.

The only remaining potential job opportunity from my first two-week job-hunting trip looked imminent. After another twenty in-person meetings during those final two weeks, I had a meeting with the Managing Director of the Charlotte office for a large, publicly traded, global consulting firm. I expected the offer to come during my last meeting of the two weeks, slated for 2:45 pm on Friday. I planned on driving back to Ohio the following day.

My heart skipped when the Managing Director started the meeting with, "You might not know this, but we've now got a hiring freeze across the company. I had to get the CEO to sign off on this position. You are the last new hire to get approved." I was dumbfounded and elated at the same time. I landed the job! I extended my stay by a day so I could put an offer on a Charlotte home on Saturday morning. How everything fell into place with no time to spare still blows me away.

Fortunately, I had seven weapons in my arsenal that I could use during my six-week "high-stakes treasure hunt," and I used each of them repeatedly. Despite the risks, that leg of my journey was exhilarating far more than it was terrifying.

EPILOGUE

"The ultimate act of surrender to God is rebellion against lies: the lies that the enemy has spoken to you, and the lies that you might have told yourself about you."

– Andrena Sawyer

From 2015 until now, the continuation of my "I planned, God laughed" career path hasn't normalized even though I'm back home in Charlotte. The firm that hired me in 2015 to eventually take over the Charlotte office had to let me go in 2017 since I didn't hit my sales target. Yep, I was unemployed again at age 55! Ugh. Since that time of unemployment, I became a partner in a business growth coaching company, a co-founder of the *Anything but Typical* podcast, and a leadership team member (and owner) of a unique, regional CPA firm focused on serving privately held business owners. Like many others, we've also endured some frightening health scares and suffered from painful family tragedies.

Through it all, I've come to appreciate the journey of life for what it is—a gift! Life is precious. Life is beautiful. Life is a journey filled with exhilarating and terrifying experiences in various environments—with unexpected detours into and out of the wilderness.

At the time of this writing, I'm 61 years young. Sixty-one years of life have given me a good bead on my Thrive/Wither zones. Yet, I still reflect regularly on my own Thrive/Wither sheet. Even at my age, I occasionally add another thing or two to my Thrive/Wither sheet.

Funny enough, I feel more alive today and better at 61 than I did at 25. I still weigh the same as I did when I was 17 competing in my first and only bodybuilding competition—Mr. Kansas. I'm stronger too—physically, spiritually, relationally, intellectually, and emotionally. Understanding the things that make me thrive and those that make me wither as part of the weapons I've used to silence the imposter are huge contributors to this. (For grins and giggles, this picture on the right was taken on my 60th birthday.)

I don't know what tomorrow holds for you or me, but as long as God grants me breath, I want to finish strong. I want to fulfill my purpose of "Doing justice, loving mercy, walking humbly with God, and making a positive difference in the lives of others." In doing so, I want to "Silence the Imposter" and unleash the "Anything but Typical" in my life. I hope this book, the Thrive/Wither exercise as part of the seven weapons we covered here, and excerpts from my story give you some inspiration and practical ways to do the same. If that hope becomes a reality, the bonus is I'm fulfilling my purpose too.

Each of us can "Silence the Imposter." Each of us can unleash "Anything but Typical." So if you've made it to the end of this book, the only thing I ask of you: please never lose sight of the fact that *you* are "Anything but Typical" by design—your unique fingerprints prove it!

Join me in celebrating the "anything but typicalness" in you and the uniqueness of others. It's one of the seven powerful weapons in your arsenal that can effectively silence the imposter.

Want to silence the imposter? It's time. It's in your control.

ABOUT THE AUTHOR

 Gary Frey is a connector, "MacGyver," and a trusted CEO confidant. He is also the co-host of the "Anything but Typical® podcast," highlighting behind-the-scenes stories of ripple-making entrepreneurs.

Throughout his career, Gary has been president of four successful companies, including Bizjournals.com. His leadership helped elevate this business news portal from a modest three-person operation to a $100 million enterprise. Gary has orchestrated two successful turnarounds and has occupied executive positions within two Fortune 500 companies.

Currently, he is an owner and spearheads business growth coaching and business development for a prominent regional CPA firm in the Southeast, serving privately held businesses and their owners.

Beyond his professional pursuits, Gary maintains an active lifestyle, regularly tackling a grueling Murph workout complete with a 20# weighted vest every Monday (for those unfamiliar, feel free to Google it!). He is also a drummer, a proud father of two accomplished sons, and a loving "Papa" to four cherished grandchildren. Gary has shared over 40 wonderful years of marriage with his devoted wife.

Gary is a prolific writer and an engaging speaker, sharing his insights on various topics relevant to entrepreneurs and organizational leaders. Some of his thought-provoking presentations include:

- **"Silence the Imposter"** (Seven Weapons for Silencing Imposter Syndrome)
- **"Why Networking Sucks & Connecting Rocks"** (Biz Dev Game-Changers)
- **"Strengths/Weaknesses isn't Enough"** (Focus on "Thrive/Wither")
- **"Core Values with Hand Grenade Impact"** (Timeless Leadership Lessons)
- **"M&A Tripwire: Cultural Incompatibility"** (Assess before the Deal)
- **"It's Hard to Read the Label When You're Inside the Jar"** (Outside perspectives)

You can connect with Gary on LinkedIn at *linkedin.com/in/garydfrey/*